About Da[...]
and *'Yma o hyd'*

CW01478545

"They'll always say we're too small, too slow, too weak, too full of fear, but *Yma o hyd*, you sons of Speed, with that Red Wall around us. We are still here. Come on, Wales. Come on." **Michael Sheen**

"[*Yma o hyd*] just puts a little bit of fire in the belly and makes me want to run a little bit more." **Conor Roberts**

"I think that whatever happens, the future of Welsh football is in safe hands, and the song will stick around, too... this tremendous symbol for how the Welsh language is now seen by Welsh people." **Elis James**

"As the World Cup hype has swept the nation, so has the respect and admiration for Dafydd [Iwan]... The tireless Welsh nationalist who served time in prison and gifted Wales its World Cup anthem."
Branwen Jones, *WalesOnline*

"[*Yma o hyd*] has snowballed into an unofficial national anthem and a slogan for the supporters, who will not hesitate to sing along."
Ben Fisher, *The Observer*

"'*Yma o hyd*' is very different to a tired old reprise of 'Sweet Caroline' or a sentimental chorus of 'football's coming home'. Instead, Iwan and the Red Wall singing in compelling union is the sound of a new Welsh confidence in its identity and language."

Donald McRae, *The Guardian*

[Dafydd Iwan] has inspired singers and songs, but he has also inspired the Welsh to think, to throw ideas around, to take action and to stand up for what they believe in. He's been doing this for 60 years, but now, in his 80th year on Earth, he's inspiring Wales more than ever. Without a doubt, the story of Welsh music would be so much poorer without his energy, his vision and his enthusiasm.

Huw Stephens

"Wales is a nation released... There is a deeper feeling of attachment from Wrexham down to Pembroke – in both the football team and national identity. They go hand in hand and at no point is that clearer than the sight of thousands singing '*Yma o hyd*', the almost 40-year-old anthem which translates to We're Still Here."

Alan Smith, *The Mirror*

"Dafydd Iwan is a Welsh icon. Synonymous with everything that is positive about Wales at the moment, he has won the hearts of every Welsh football fan... The resurrection of '*Yma o hyd*', Iwan's folk anthem about the Welsh people and language, has reinvigorated a nation."

Christopher Evans, *Nation.Cymru*

DAFYDD IWAN

STILL SINGING
'YMA O HYD'

AN AUTOBIOGRAPHY

First impression: 2023

© Copyright Dafydd Iwan and Y Lolfa Cyf., 2023

The contents of this book are subject to copyright, and may
not be reproduced by any means, mechanical or electronic,
without the prior, written consent of the publishers.

The publishers wish to acknowledge
the support of the Books Council of Wales.

Cover design: Y Lolfa
Cover image: FAWales and John Smith

ISBN: 978 1 912631 49 0

Published and printed in Wales
on paper from well-maintained forests by
Y Lolfa Cyf., Talybont, Ceredigion SY24 5HE
website www.ylolfa.com
e-mail ylolfa@ylolfa.com
tel 01970 832 304

Contents

Foreword

IN MY FIRST year at Eirias High School in Colwyn Bay, our English teacher John Price gave us the task of writing about two individuals who had influenced us. This was a period of emergence in terms of Welsh awareness and identity, politically and with regard to the Welsh language. At the heart of the movement was Dafydd Iwan, in terms of popular culture and messaging through his songs. It was a period of understanding why there was so little public recognition of the language. I chose to write about him as one of the people who had influenced me.

The second was my first footballing hero: Roger Hunt, the legendary Liverpool player. He was a part of Bill Shankly's first great Liverpool side. He was the club's record goal scorer with 286 and is regarded as one of Liverpool's greatest ever players. I saw him play live, saw him score goals and wanted to be like him.

Football and Welsh history coming together in the early 1970s. Little did I know at the time how important both would still be to me nearly 50 years later, ahead of Wales qualifying for their first World Cup Finals since 1958.

At the end of the World Cup qualifying campaign, in the matches against both Belarus and Belgium, as the players did their lap of honour, the crowd spontaneously sang 'Yma o hyd'. A song that had been around the Welsh men's squad for a few years and had been prominent on the players' playlist.

Ahead of the Austria play-off semi-final planning meeting at the Cardiff City Stadium, every potential advantage was discussed – including the pre-match atmosphere. A suggestion was made that to get the crowd involved just ahead of the players coming onto the field, Dafydd Iwan should perform live.

No one really could have predicted what would happen when he did.

The singing throughout the whole stadium, the reaction and the impact – and of course the exercise was repeated for the Ukraine match, to even greater effect.

The effect, the impact was powerful. On the Thursday following qualification, Dafydd was invited to meet the squad at the team hotel. Their reaction, the respect shown towards him was huge: real recognition from a group of young men about the contribution Dafydd and 'Yma o hyd' had made to their success on the field. They understood, like so many, that this was about more than football.

Dafydd's contribution to Wales is far greater than 'Yma o hyd'. As he himself also says: "I do have other songs!"

I'm sure he would admit that he never envisaged that a song composed in 1983 would have such an impact over 40 years later on a world stage.

And that moment ahead of and at the end of the Ukraine game will forever be a part of Welsh history.

Ian Gwyn Hughes
October 2023

Preface

IT WAS THURSDAY, 24 March 2022, and I was on my way to sing before Wales' match against Austria in our journey towards the World Cup in Qatar. I was full of trepidation, as my previous experiences of such performances had not gone too well. The atmosphere was building up, and the whole of Wales, it seemed, was making its way to the City Stadium in Caerdydd. There was a growing feeling of confidence in the air, even though we'd been here before, of course! Yet there was something different this time, and what I didn't know was that this night would change my life.

I made my way to the platform under the Canton Stand, under the watchful direction of Dave Driscoll. I stood before the microphone, knowing that Dave had ensured everything was working well and the sound quality would be great. But I still had my doubts. What if the Red Wall didn't respond? What if I ended up singing on my own? As the team finished their pre-game kickabout, I was given the nod. The track began playing. I was terrified and full of excited confidence all at the same time.

I needn't have worried! The Red Wall joined in, and almost knocked me off the platform with the power of their singing as they turned up the volume for the chorus. It was truly amazing – beyond anything I had experienced in 60 years of singing. And the song I had sung for almost 40 years suddenly came truly alive, and filled the City Stadium with the spirit and emotion of a reborn Cymru. Ian Gwyn Hughes' idea had come of age, with a vengeance!

If you watch the video on YouTube, you'll see the tears streaming down my face. It was an astounding, emotional moment for me. But as I said, this happened six decades into my career as a singer and activist. How had events conspired to bring me to this performance on this day?

Let me go back to the beginning.

CHAPTER 1

Brynaman (1943–1955)

I WAS BORN in Brynaman as the Second World War was drawing to its bloody close, and the war left its mark on all our lives. I think I have a vague memory of spending the night in an air-raid shelter, packed in with the rest of my family and neighbours, but I was only a baby, and can never be absolutely sure about this. After all, such memories tended to be recalled for years after the war ended, and I suppose they can easily become part of a shared experience where fact and fiction become confused. But the bombing of Swansea was real, and certainly a topic of intense discussion for many years, and the remains of the German plane on the Black Mountain above the village was real enough.

As children, we joined in with the gang marching down Bryn Avenue, armed with wooden swords and cardboard battledress, chanting, *"We won the war in nineteen-forty-four,"* as we prepared to meet the enemy – the 'Banwen Japs' – on the bridge over the Aman. The 'Banwen Japs' was our name for those who lived in Lower Brynaman – rather offensive now, but obviously this was just after the war and all its anti-Japanese propaganda. The first thing you must remember about Brynaman is that it is split into two – Upper and Lower. We lived in Upper Brynaman, north of the Aman River, in Carmarthenshire, and the enemy lived in Lower Brynaman, also known as Banwen, in Glamorganshire. And never the twain shall meet – except in war!

The other big difference the war made to our lives was the rationing, which didn't disappear completely until 1954. It meant we couldn't buy sweets in the shop by the school. And I remember that wonderful day when sweet rations were lifted at last, and I could go to the shop and actually use the sixpenny piece which had lain useless in my pocket for so long to buy a bar of Bounty. Oh, glorious day! But the ecstasy soon subsided as the sixpenny pieces in my pocket seemed to become more scarce.

Brynaman was a coal-mining village in those days, situated as it was on the western fringe of the great south Wales coalfield. There were several mines in the area, and some of the best anthracite coal around was mined in the Aman Valley. Most of my schoolfriends were either the children of colliers or closely related to colliers, and one scene which remains a vivid memory is that of the miners returning from the early shift, their faces black, and the clatter of their hobnailed boots ringing in my ears. Clinging to our garden gate, I watched that scene transfixed, and marvelled at these wonderful men who spent half their lives deep underground so that we could get coal. That coal arrived in our house, courtesy of an arrangement with the chapel where my father was a minister, dumped outside the gate.

Our house was fairly large, and owned by Gibea, the chapel which employed my father. I always remember it as a cold house, however hard my father worked on keeping the coal fire burning in the grate. It's probably true to say that an open fire in a small grate, where most of the heat goes up the chimney, is one of the least efficient ways of heating a room, but my father took great pride spending time in the morning cleaning the grates (we had two fires going when we could afford it) and setting the fire for the evening. He wore a beret for this job, and he would also enjoy making coal pellets from coaldust and cement, fashioned with a contraption designed by one of the chapel deacons, who was a blacksmith in a local colliery. Dad used to love pottering about like this – another of his favourite DIY projects was carving rubber soles for our clogs from old car tyres. Gardening was his other great love – always wearing his beret. Then, after completing his chores, he would wash, change into something more ministerial, and go into his study to work on a sermon, or leave home for a visit to an ailing chapel member, or a funeral, or a hospital visit. I was always slightly envious of my friends who had real coal miners as fathers, and they always looked at my brothers and me as rather strange beings.

There were four of us: Huw Ceredig, me, Arthur Morus, and – a few years later – Alun Ffred. Being the sons of a preacher, we had no choice on Sunday but to go to chapel, three times usually: the morning service, where we recited a verse from the Bible; Sunday School after dinner; and the evening service at 6 p.m. Then during the week there was the Band of Hope on Tuesday, and sometimes another meeting where we rehearsed songs for the eisteddfod, or the Christmas drama. An eisteddfod (a cultural festival with competitions) was held in each of the six chapels in Brynaman, where the prize was a penny in a small knitted pouch hung around our necks, and the winners went on to the big eisteddfod in the Public Hall. That event filled the Hall (which doubled as a cinema – and still does to this day) and went on for three days, and it was there that I first tasted those dreaded pre-stage nerves and the drug-like magic of audience applause.

A mere stone's throw from our house in Bryn Avenue was the cricket field, where we spent many a happy hour, watching the village team, playing ourselves on the fringes after school, or tumbling in the sweet-smelling newly mown grass. People are somewhat surprised when they hear of my love of cricket, that most English and most boring of games, but in Brynaman, apart from the seasonal marbles and conkers, there were two games played: rugby in winter, and cricket in summer, and both were taken very seriously indeed. My other great sporting interest – and I will say this in hushed tones – was boxing. I had heard stories of the Welsh legends of the ring (fighters like Tommy Farr, Freddie Welsh, Jim Driscoll, Jimmy Wilde, and Jack Petersen), but the later ones – Dai Dower, Joe Erskine and Howard Winstone – became my boyhood heroes. I used to run across the road to see Welsh amateur boxers on TV, and have my ears glued to the radio, listening to championship fights. But two experiences helped to quell my interest in this fascinating but cruel sport: one was being present in

Winstone's last fight in Porthcawl, when the great boxer had lost his guile and was completely outclassed by José Legrá from Cuba, and the second was seeing my hero Joe Erskine working as a bouncer at a night club in Tiger Bay: a bumbling giant, hardly able to speak.

But rugby was Brynaman's game – which explains why I still consider it to be my first love, despite its present problems, and despite my close links with 'soccer' recently and the fact that my sons are very much into the round-ball game. R C C (Clem) Thomas was a Brynaman boy, and R H Williams lived in Cwmllynfell, close enough for us to claim him as one of ours. On our street there was a family of talented rugby players – John Elgar Williams played for Llanelli, his brother Ellis Wyn played for London Welsh and Eurfyl also shone on the field. And there are a number of Brynaman boys who made a name for themselves as rugby commentators – Alun Wyn Bevan, who graduated from being a first-class referee to being a first-class TV presenter; Alun Tudur Jenkins, who for many years was a commentator for the BBC on horse-racing and rugby; and just beyond the boundary of Lower Brynaman were the homes of the Welsh voice of rugby, Huw Llywelyn Davies, and probably the best rugby player of them all, Gareth Edwards.

And since I am in the mood for name-dropping, a little further down the Aman valley was the home of the great Shane Williams (my claim to fame is that we were born in the same Glanaman hospital, albeit a few decades apart), and as I'm writing this, the Wales rugby team is doing very well in the Rugby World Cup in France, and the captain is a Brynaman boy: Jac Morgan, a player to inspire a nation. Not content with the men's team, the village has also supplied the captain of the Wales women's rugby team, Hannah Jones. Brynaman at the forefront again!

Brynaman was – and still is to a lesser degree – a thoroughly Welsh and Welsh-speaking village. Cymraeg, spoken in a beautiful and rather unique accent, was the natural first language of the colliers and their families, and everything to do with the chapel was conducted in Welsh. Welsh was the predominant language on the school playground, as well as on the rugby and cricket field, but the lessons in the primary school were a mix of Welsh and English, with English gradually coming to the fore as you progressed through the years, until everyone was expected to sit the hated 'eleven-plus' exam through the medium of English. But a few parents – like my own – insisted that we should sit it in Welsh. Apparently, I was one of only three or four pupils who entered the Amman Valley Grammar School in 1954 who had sat the exam in Welsh. And that was my first experience of being in a radical minority.

But the biggest traumatic culture shock was arriving at the school itself and finding that my language was practically non-existent! I still spoke it with my friends, of course, but the lessons were all in English – with the sole exception of the Welsh lesson itself – the teachers all spoke to us in English, and the morning assembly and every other formal school activity were all conducted in English. I have never felt so excluded in my own country. And the fact which illustrates the power of the anglicised system we were subjected to better than any other is that, years later, we found that most of the teachers were in fact Welsh speakers themselves. But they were engulfed by the English educational machine, and totally subservient to it. (Of course, there were notable exceptions, like the late Meurig Evans: there always are, thank God.)

I am often asked why I 'became' a Welsh Nationalist, and my answer is that I was born into it. I don't recall my parents going on about it, but to them, to support everything Welsh was the most natural thing in the world, and that meant supporting all Welsh sporting teams and Plaid Cymru, and everything between. My grandfather on my father's side was one of the founding members of Plaid Cymru; my mother came from a staunch Liberal-supporting farming family from Montgomeryshire; but both of them became members of Plaid in their teens.

My own first taste of party politics was the 1955 General Election, when Jennie Eirian Davies stood for Plaid in Carmarthenshire. She was the wife of Upper Brynaman's Methodist minister Eirian Davies, and lived directly opposite us in Bryn Avenue. Jennie was an eloquent orator and a very persuasive candidate, but the strength of support for Labour in that coal-mining village meant that she stood no chance at all. Indeed, the fact that both Eirian Davies and my father were openly supportive of Plaid Cymru created many problems for them in their respective chapels, where the deacons and elders were, almost to a man, Labour to the core. It is little wonder that Labour was seen as the party of the working class, and Plaid as the party of preachers, poets and teachers. But what I learned from those preachers – including my father – in their pulpits was about the struggle of the people of South Africa against the apartheid regime, the campaigns against nuclear arms and the war in Vietnam. Whatever the Labour supporters believed and said, those 'nasty, narrow-minded' Nashy preachers opened our eyes to the international fight against oppression everywhere, and to the global struggle for freedom and peace.

Before I leave Brynaman and the Amman Valley Grammar School, one incident stands out in my mind, which was probably my first real revolutionary act – and my first brush with the Royal Establishment. One morning, as we settled in our seats at the start of another day of English education, we noticed a large new poster of Queen Elizabeth staring out at us from the noticeboard. I believe it may have been a poster advertising National Savings. A few of us decided that it would be a great idea to embellish the poster with a few artistic additions, and during the lunchbreak, we gave our sovereign lady a patch over one eye, a grand moustache, a pipe in her mouth and a pair of specs. I cannot be certain which of these was my contribution, but we all agreed that they gave the poster some added power.

But of course, the authorities took a different view, and we were ordered to own up – which we did, much to our credit. We were summoned to the headmaster's office, shaking with the nervous fear of the unknown. As we entered that hallowed place, the headmaster (a rather short, rounded man) looked as if he was about to burst, his face red as a tomato. He held the decorated poster as high as he could muster, and shouted, as if he was in a Shakespeare play, "THIS IS OUR QUEEN!!!"

I don't remember much after that, only that I had to pinch myself as hard as I could, in the hope the pain would be stronger than my overpowering urge to burst out laughing. We were all given a suitable punishment, and warned that if we ever did anything of the sort again, we would be banished for life.

CHAPTER 2

Llanuwchllyn
(1955–1966)

IN 1955, MY father accepted the position of Minister at Yr Hen Gapel in Llanuwchllyn, Meirionnydd. It was an offer he could not refuse, for Llanuwchllyn, and the chapel itself, had a pedigree which could hardly be surpassed. Some of the biggest names in Welsh national and cultural history from the previous hundred years were linked to this place: Sir Owen M Edwards, who many believe was the founder of popular Welsh literature; his son Sir Ifan, founder of Urdd Gobaith Cymru, the Welsh youth movement; and Michael D Jones, one of the movers behind the Welsh colony in Patagonia. Côr Godre'r Aran, one of the most outstanding – and longest surviving – Welsh male voice choirs, was based in the village under their pioneering leader Tom Jones, and Ifor Owen, father of the first Welsh-language comic, was the inspiring headteacher in the local school. And if that was not enough of an attraction, the area was blessed with Wales' largest natural lake, Llyn Tegid, the mountains of Aran and Arennig, the Celtic fortress of Carndochan and the Roman fort of Caer Gai.

My father was inaugurated in the chapel on a misty day in late autumn. And when I say misty, I mean visibility down to a few yards, and I can hardly recollect another fog like it during the ten years I called Llanuwchllyn home. I remember sitting in the bus which had brought the congregation of Gibea, Brynaman up for the occasion and which was now taking us to the chapel. The two ladies sitting in front of me, who were already aghast at the idea of Mr Jones moving all this way 'up north' from Brynaman, were looking out of the window and seeing absolutely nothing but a thick wet fog, and one said to the other, *"Beth ddath dros ei ben e yn symud i shwt le?* (Whatever came over him to move to such a place?)"

But the fog soon cleared, and we grew to love our new home and its people. We obviously missed Brynaman and the friendly warmth of the coal-mining culture, but Llanuwchllyn offered a new kind of warmth, that of a farming community rich in history and alive with an active, creative Welsh-language culture. Indeed, in Brynaman and Llanuwchllyn, I became aware of the breadth of the Welsh way of life in two areas of Wales which were a hundred miles apart, but belonging to the same cultural tradition.

If rugby and cricket had been the games at Brynaman, Llanuwchllyn was strictly football, and not an oval ball in sight. Having said that, I made it into the school cricket XI, but that was mainly down to the fact that the school was short of able-bodied boys who had some sort of idea what to do with a bat and ball, and my cricketing career was not a glorious one. But football was big in Llan and in Bala, and my younger brother Alun Ffred later became a fixture as the goalie for Llan. It was his experiences there that gave him the inspiration for the popular radio – and later TV – comedy series *C'mon Midffild*, which he co-wrote and produced during the 1980s.

I was 12 when we moved to Llanuwchllyn, so I missed out on the chance to experience the teaching skills of Ifor Owen and went straight to Ysgol Tŷ Tan Domen, the school for boys at Bala, housed in an ageing stone building on the edge of town. The most memorable aspect of my Bala schooldays has nothing to do with education, however – it was the journey by train from Llanuwchllyn along the shores of Llyn Tegid every morning and afternoon. This was before Beeching vandalised our rail system, when trains were still running from Corwen and beyond through to Dolgellau and Barmouth, and from Bala to Trawsfynydd, Porthmadog and Blaenau Ffestiniog. But our school train was very special – just one solitary coach, and no corridor. And it was run like a local bus, stopping at every possible stop, and even waiting for stragglers on the way. And the lake was something else – looking different every day, sometimes stormy, sometimes like a mirror to the surrounding hills, a thing of beauty which even carefree schoolchildren could not fail to appreciate. I doubt whether there was a better school run anywhere in the world.

The school authorities for some reason decided that I could skip a year and join the third-year students at Bala, and this, combined with the fact that my birthday was in late August, meant I was the youngest in my class by some distance. This had two major results: the first was that I was the first boy in the school's history to be still wearing short trousers in the sixth form, and the second was that I was destined to sit some form of significant exams every summer for the next ten years! It started with O levels, some fourteen subjects spread over three summers, and then four A level subjects spread over a further three summers. I stayed on for a year at Bala as I was deemed to be too young to go to university, and eventually found my way to Aberystwyth. But by then I had decided to study Architecture, mainly because I believed Welsh students were too confined to the traditional paths in education, and did not venture into more adventurous fields. I had also learnt that Dewi-Prys Thomas was to be the Head of the Welsh School of Architecture in Cardiff, and that added to the appeal of the subject as I had heard he was an inspiring lecturer at the Liverpool School of Architecture.

However, to study for a degree in Architecture at that time meant that you had first to 'prove' yourself academically by studying three subjects for a year in one of the constituent colleges of the University of Wales. I was the last to be subjected to this strange regime, and by the time I arrived in Cardiff, the Architecture degree course had been changed to include courses at the University College in Cardiff. So I studied (a very loose term in this context) Welsh, English and Art at Aberystwyth, and Economic History, Art and Archaeology in Cardiff. My year at Aberystwyth, however, had more to do with sampling the delights of the town's vast array of pubs, and helping to stir the revolutionary waters that led to the forming of Cymdeithas yr Iaith Gymraeg the following year.

Cymdeithas yr Iaith Gymraeg (literally 'The Welsh Language Society') is probably the most significant movement to be formed in Wales during the second half of the twentieth century. It grew out of the cauldron of the Sixties, when young people throughout the Western hemisphere believed we could change the world. There were huge rallies against apartheid, against the Vietnam war, against nuclear arms, and for civil rights in North America. There were radical student revolts on the European continent, and Northern Ireland was beginning to boil over.

As the smaller nations of Europe found their own voices, Cymru too was stirring with a new spirit of independence. Cymdeithas was formed following a passionate BBC lecture on the future of the Welsh language by the veteran nationalist poet, dramatist and academic Saunders Lewis, and its first goal was to secure full official recognition for the Welsh language. Until 1967, the Welsh language had no official status in its own country, and Cymdeithas set about the task of challenging the authorities to use Cymraeg on all official forms, signs and documents, and to allow the use of Cymraeg in courts of law. The difference between the methods used by Cymdeithas and previous campaigns was that the members were prepared, if all other methods had failed, to use direct action and civil disobedience to achieve its aims, even if that meant facing prison sentences. This was a major development, and it has, over more than 60 years of continuous campaigning, achieved significant results. And while most other movements set up in the Sixties have faded, Cymdeithas is still going strong!

During my rather inglorious year at Aberystwyth, I achieved the dual distinction of the top marks in Welsh and the lowest marks in English, and much edification in the lectures of R L Gapper in the History of Art. But the summer following that year saw the beginnings of my life as a singer-songwriter. Leaving for university, of course, means that your ties with home are weakened, even severed. I missed Llanuwchllyn, but when I returned home over the summer, I worked at the Urdd centre at Glan-llyn, and it was there that I learnt a few chords on the guitar and started to sing simple songs to entertain the campers. Little did I know then that I was laying the foundations to an activity which was to become one of the major pillars of my life.

The songs I sang to begin with were adaptations of American folk songs, mainly from the *Burl Ives Song Book*. The melodies were simple, mostly within reach of the few guitar chords I had managed to master, and I put Welsh words to them. 'Froggy Went A-Courtin'' became *'Gee ceffyl bach'*, 'Shucking of the Corn' became *'Meddwl amdanat ti'*, and Woody Guthrie's classic 'This Land Is Your Land' became *'Mae'n wlad i mi'*. Such simply strummed ditties would not get much reaction from today's teenagers, but the effect they had on the Urdd campers of the mid Sixties is difficult to explain. Many a night, they refused to go to bed until I gave *'Gee ceffyl bach'* another go, and I was rather overwhelmed by it all. Teenagers since those innocent days have been swept away by the growth of rock 'n' roll in all its forms, and subjected to a continuous succession of popular music through an increasing array of media platforms.

But in 1964, I was beginning to savour the strange taste of popularity!

In the background to all this, while I was fumbling for new chords on the guitar and trying my hand at writing lyrics, the campaigns of Cymdeithas were gathering pace, and many members appeared in court as a result. And in 1965, after years of protest and despite the opposition of all Welsh MPs bar one, the Tryweryn dam was opened, leading to the drowning of the Welsh-speaking community of Capel Celyn to provide water for industry in the Liverpool area. Over the years, this event has achieved a political significance like no other, and has come to symbolise the inability of Wales to defend its own resources, and to receive adequate recompense for resources taken from Wales. The graffiti on a wall near Llanrhystud in Ceredigion, *Cofiwch Dryweryn* ('Remember Tryweryn'), is now seen on car stickers and school walls throughout Wales, as we become more aware of the need to have more control over our lives as Welsh people. The name Tryweryn crops up in many songs, including my own.

Things developed apace with my singing, which left architecture a distant second (not a great loss to the world of architecture, I might add!). One day the late John Edwards – a pioneer of the Welsh recording industry – called in at my student digs on West Cowbridge Road and offered me the chance to record an EP. I remember telling him, half in jest, that I had only just mastered my third guitar chord (which has become a running gag throughout my career!), and felt I needed more time to prepare my songs and improve my guitar playing. But he was adamant that I "had something", especially the song I had recently sung on the TWW (Television Wales and West) programme *Y Dydd* (The Day), which was a political commentary on my attitude to Wales: '*Wrth feddwl am fy Nghymru*' (As I think of Wales). In that song, the first I had written both words and music to, I outlined the four pillars of my nationalism – Wales' history, the Welsh language, the drowning of Tryweryn, and how it was our turn now to right the wrongs of the past. From today's perspective, it seems strange that I was asked to sing such a political song on what was, after all, a news magazine show, but in those days, I was merely an idealistic student dreaming about an improbable future. Plaid Cymru was a mere sideshow with no real power, and Cymdeithas yr Iaith a Welsh manifestation of the Sixties protest generation. I was topical, but not to be taken too seriously. However, as it happened, that song had far-reaching repercussions.

The story of the early years of the fledgling Welsh recording industry was similar to the story of Welsh chapels, with one label continually splitting from another. John Edwards had been employed by the Talfan Davies family to run the pioneering Qualiton label in Pontardawe, and when they decided to sell out to Decca, John was so incensed that in 1962 he set up his own label – Welsh Teldisc, taking Josia (Jo) Jones with him from Pontardawe. But Jo soon upped sticks and founded the Cambrian label, which mopped up most Welsh singers until the mid Seventies, while the son of one of the Talfan brothers set up the Dryw (Wren) publishers and record label in Llandybie in 1964, run by Dennis Rees.

But in 1966, Jo Jones was still working for Welsh Teldisc, and it was he who took us to the Crynant Social Club one Sunday morning to record my first EP. The recording engineer was Noel Kendrick from Clydach, an amateur who knew his stuff, but who was working with very basic equipment – a Ferrograph tape recorder on a trestle table and a couple of microphones. When I had decided to accept John Edwards' offer, I phoned my friend Edward (Morus Jones), who had been in a band with my brother Arthur in Llanuwchllyn, to ask if he would mind doing some backing vocals and playing his 12-string guitar on the EP. Edward agreed with his usual enthusiasm, and we set about the recording, albeit with some trepidation. However, things went so well that within an hour or so Jo was asking us whether we had another four songs for another EP!

We scrambled around for a bit, and decided we had three songs more or less ready, and Edward remembered he had a Welsh adaptation of Woody Guthrie's 'This Land Is My Land' somewhere. He searched his car but to no avail, and the words never came to light, so we decided to write our own there and then. So was born our version of *'Mae'n wlad i mi'* (It's my country), which has been sung a thousand times all over Wales over the past 60 years and more. I am intrigued by Woody Guthrie, a migrant labourer who travelled widely in America with his guitar, and wrote songs describing his travels and his thoughts about America. This was during the Great Depression, and many of Woody's songs call upon the American government to invest in the future rather than continue with the cuts which meant so much hardship to ordinary workers. His most celebrated song, 'This Land Is My Land', is not merely a song of praise to America, but a commentary on the sight of people queuing for food handouts in a land so full of wealth. His son, in his memoirs, says that the original draft of the song included the line "God made this land for you and me", and I was fascinated to find that my great-grandfather, Jeremiah Jones of Y Cilie in Llangrannog, was renowned for his political ballads, and one of these included the lines:

Rhoer daear i'r gweithiwr fel gallo gael byw –
Nid daear i'r Landlord fwriadwyd gan Dduw

(Give the land to the worker so he may live
God did not make the land for the Landlord)

This was written 54 years before Woody Guthrie wrote his anthem, and I feel so proud to be a part of such a rich and important tradition!

When Edward and I made that first recording in Crynant, I was still in the early period of original songwriting, so many of the tracks on those two first EPs were adaptations of American folk songs:

TEP 861 (1966): *'Wrth feddwl am fy Nghymru'*, *'Wyt ti'n cofio?'* (Do you remember?), *'Bryniau Bro Afallon'* (The hills of Bro Afallon – aka 'Big Rock Candy Mountain'), *'Meddwl amdanat ti'* (Thinking of you – aka 'Shucking of the Corn')

TEP 864 (1966): *'Mae'n wlad i mi'* (It's my country – aka 'This Land Is Your Land'), *'Gee ceffyl bach'* (Gee little horse

– aka 'Froggy Went A-Courtin'), *'Crwydro'* (Wandering
– aka 'Silver Threads Among the Gold'), *'Mae'r esgid fach yn gwasgu'* (The little shoe is pinching).

Thereafter, almost all the songs I have recorded have been of my own making, but this was the beginning of my recording career and I was very much feeling my way into new and unknown territories.

That was in 1966, the year my father accepted an invitation to be minister of two small chapels on the Caerfyrddin-Ceredigion border; he was gradually making his way back to the land of his forebears in Llangrannog. In the meantime, I had spent six years 'in exile' in Caerdydd, and many of the songs I wrote in that period were full of *hiraeth* for Llanuwchllyn and rural Welsh Wales. *Hiraeth* is one of those Welsh words which cannot be fully translated, and is very close to what could be called the 'soul' or 'psyche' of Cymru. It is a mix of nostalgia and longing – for that which is lost forever, or for that which is yet to come; in songs, it is often a longing for people or places left behind, or the longing of those left behind for those who have gone. But my *hiraeth* had been eased somewhat by the campaigns of Cymdeithas yr Iaith. I missed their first protest, on Trefechan Bridge, and the court cases following the bomb set by Mudiad Amddiffyn Cymru activists at the Tryweryn Dam site, as I was stuck in Caerdydd, but I promised myself that I would not miss another protest or campaign for the language and for Wales. As far as I was concerned, the fight-back – after generations, if not centuries, of being second-class citizens in our own country – had begun, and I knew I had to be a part of it. And for the next 15 years, my life was dedicated to that cause.

There were two major occurrences in 1966 which underlined, in very different ways, how Wales was changing, and why things had to change. In July Gwynfor Evans won the Caerfyrddin seat for Plaid Cymru in a stirring by-election, giving Plaid Cymru their very first MP, and the politics of Wales was changed for ever. And in October 144 people, including 116 children, were engulfed by a coal-waste avalanche in Aberfan – despite the National Coal Board having been warned about the risks of dumping coal slurry on a site above the school – and Wales was left grieving once more, and the people of Wales asking ourselves when the suffering of working Welsh families would end.

My regular TV appearances on TWW (and later HTV), and the records, combined with some notoriety as a prominent member of the language protests of Cymdeithas yr Iaith, made me a 'household name' in Welsh-speaking communities, and the invitations to sing in various villages throughout Wales came in ever-increasing numbers. I had bought a little A35 van for the travelling, but there was one slight problem – I hadn't passed my driving test, so I had to badger the drivers amongst my friends to accompany me on my journeys. These could, of course, be journeys to the far corners of Wales, and meant returning to Caerdydd in the early hours of the following morning. Generally, my friends were very accommodating, but I have to admit, from this safe distance, that I did have to venture on a few occasions without a co-driver when all attempts to persuade my friends had failed. I particularly remember one journey to the West when I was accompanied by a friend (who later became a prominent civil servant in the Welsh Office, and subsequently the Welsh Assembly), and he was known to be very proud of his car and his clean driving licence. Fair play to him, he agreed to come with me "just this once", probably against his better judgement. All went well until, with my co-driver asleep beside me, I was stopped by the police on Stormy Down near Penybont on my way home for exceeding the speed limit for a van with no side windows. I was subsequently fined, but the one who had the points on his licence was my sleeping friend and co-driver. He went to his grave, poor man, without ever fully forgiving me!

Anyway, I eventually passed my driving test on my fourth attempt (I always explained this as being due to having developed driving habits which did not always conform to the Highway Code while driving for so long without passing), and my journeys throughout Wales continued to multiply. These were to small village halls or chapel vestries, where I would have to sit for hours on dusty chairs waiting for my turn, as the fashion of the day was to have a long string of singers, reciters and comics to fill the bill. Later, as the world of Welsh-language pop began to expand, I would perform in larger venues, such as the huge Pontrhydfendigaid Pavilion, in the extravaganzas which became very popular for a while.

I didn't have an agent, and I had no idea what I should charge, so for many years I asked for a few pounds, which hardly covered my petrol expenses. As the years passed, I gradually gained more confidence in asking a more reasonable fee, but as most Welsh-language artists are technically 'amateur' (it's hard to make a living from Welsh-language singing alone), there has always been a sense that singing in Welsh is something we should do out of the goodness of our hearts rather than work we do for financial gain. Indeed, over the 60 years or more I have been doing this, that has been the most significant development – seeing Welsh culture gradually and painfully emerging from what was essentially an amateur, unpaid way of life to the quasi-professional situation we have today. But having said that, probably 90% of my singing engagements over the years have been in aid of some 'good cause' or other – patching a leaky roof on the chapel or village hall, raising money for the never-ending round of local and national eisteddfodau, Plaid and Cymdeithas, children's playgrounds and sports teams, or any of the rich plethora of community activities which make life in Wales so interesting. It all adds to the dilemma of the aspiring Welsh performer!

CHAPTER 3

Protest, Business, Marriage and Prison (1968–1982)

ON 1 JANUARY 1968, I married Marion, the daughter of a slate quarryman in Mynydd Llandegai, a village overlooking Bethesda and its famous Penrhyn slate quarry. Later that year, I graduated as a Bachelor of Architecture in Caerdydd, and, after years of participating in a string of rallies, marches, sit-ins and protests of all kinds, mainly to gain full official status for the Welsh language, I was elected Chair of Cymdeithas yr Iaith in October 1968. It was the beginning of what was to be probably the most dramatic and high-profile period of language campaigning. 1 January 1969 saw the start of the road-sign-painting campaign, accompanied by a myriad court-cases and many imprisonments. Before then, most official road signs in Wales were in English only, and if Welsh placenames were included, they were often spelt incorrectly. After years of fruitless petitions, rallies and meetings, the new painting campaign saw hundreds of young people throughout Wales painting over English road signs with green paint, and of course, the public response was often immediate, vociferous and bad-tempered. This was followed by a year's moratorium, followed by the taking down of signs all over Wales. And on top of all this came the Investiture of Charles, an English prince descended from the royal line that had subjugated Wales and made laws to try to stamp out our language, as 'Prince of Wales'. To a nationalist singer-songwriter, this was manna from heaven; to a language campaigner, it was a dangerous 'hospital-pass'.

In fact, I spoke in the General Meeting of Cymdeithas yr Iaith in October 1968 against making too much of our opposition to the Investiture, instead recommending that we stick to our main task of securing full official status for the Welsh language. The first Welsh Language Act of 1967 had been something of a damp squib. It set in law the principle of 'equal validity' between Welsh and English, and gave people the right to use Welsh in a court of law, but it was a long way from what we were campaigning for. However, it was a start, and it gave us a yearning for more. But try as we might, the juggernaut of the Investiture rolled in and took over the airwaves, and for a year or so, we became not the champions of the language, but the opposition to the Prince's party. The Investiture promised the people of Wales "three months of great celebrations", and we were the party poopers.

I wrote an innocent little tongue-in-cheek ditty portraying Charles as the greatest Welshman on earth, and it became the focus of much bile and hatred. I received a torrent of anonymous letters and death-threats, and I once received a carefully packaged parcel through the post, containing human excrement. Our local paper

35

in Caernarfon – especially the Welsh language version, *Yr Herald Cymraeg* – under the editor John Eilian (a crowned national bard, no less) likened my voice to that of a lovesick seal, and encouraged everyone to boycott the record as a "hymn of hate". Of course, with that kind of publicity, the record sold by the thousands, and the *Herald* was duty-bound to publish the local Top Ten they had pioneered, with 'Carlo' as their Number One!

The language campaigns had to take a back seat while all this royal circus was going on, and Wales – especially Welsh-speaking Wales – became for a while a seething sea of argument, rifts and splits. Together with the furore caused by the road-signs campaign, the political temperature in Wales was close to boiling, and rose still further when members of the Free Wales Army, a nationalist group who made dramatic appearances in paramilitary uniforms and who many thought were responsible for bombings carried out around this time, were sentenced to lengthy jail sentences on the very day of the Investiture itself. They were tense times, and it was probably the period of my life when I most bore the full blast of public opposition in all its forms. But there was also a strong well of support, and a growing sense that Wales was somehow waking up to a new reality – a new kind of national feeling, free of servility and grovelling in the shadow of a dying British Empire.

For me, 1969 was not only a year of protest and political argument, it was also the year when Huw Jones and I set up the Sain record label. We had both been recording for the Swansea-based Welsh Teldisc label, and the two singles I released in 1969 – 'Carlo' and '*Croeso chwedeg* nain' (a dig at the Investiture celebrations) – had both been big sellers. But Huw and I felt that it was time the Welsh recording scene moved on and took advantage of the new technology The Beatles and others had developed, and we tried to persuade Welsh Teldisc to invest in some new equipment. But to no avail. John Edwards had recently died and his widow was thinking of retirement, and was content to keep on packing more of the singles I had recorded. She was very nice about it, and wished Huw and me the best with our plans. We eventually found a willing partner in Brian Morgan Edwards, a young Tory who had converted to Plaid Cymru, who worked for IBM and had recently moved from London to Caerdydd. He gave us £500, a filing cabinet and a phone in his front room in Ninian Road, bought a company off the shelf, and set us on our way.

Huw was already working on a new single, 'Dŵr', and this became Sain's first release. It was a song about the drowning of a valley to provide water for an English city, and it was inspired by what had happened recently in Tryweryn and Clywedog, where another community had been evicted and their valley drowned to supply water to the West Midlands. The track featured a variety of instruments, and backing vocals by Heather Jones, and it set the tone for Sain's releases during the 1970s – strong political messaging, robust singing and instrumentation and use of state-of-the-art technology. Huw had used various studios in Wales, London and Bristol, but we then settled for the famous Rockfield Studios in Monmouth, until we set up our own studio in a converted cowshed at Gwernafalau, Llandwrog in 1974.

1971 was the year a group of us young nationalists became very worried about the rapid expansion of second homes, climbing clubs and weekend cottages in Eryri and the Llŷn Peninsula. We looked around for a possible answer to this growing problem, which mopped up houses that could have been homes for locals, and once again, Brian Morgan Edwards came up with a suggestion. He helped us to set up Cymdeithas Tai Gwynedd, the first rural-based housing association in England and Wales. The plan was simple – raising money from the public in the form of Loan Stock, buying terraced houses in the villages affected, using local council renovation grants to improve them, and letting them at a reasonable rent to locals.

Many people in the housing and banking industries warned us that it wouldn't work, and advised us to give it up. But we stuck at it and today, Cymdeithas Tai Gwynedd has over 30 properties worth nearly five million pounds, each one a home for a local family. Despite rapidly rising costs, our rents are still affordable. We have resisted all attempts to make us an 'official' housing association as we want to remain in charge of our own policy regarding where to buy and who we can rent to – although we did set up a sister association, Tai Eryri, which could benefit from Government funding and which later joined forces with Tai Clwyd, and is now a part of the north Wales-wide Grwp Cynefin. But we remain independent, and proud of it. Meanwhile, alas, the housing crisis goes on.

I've skipped over some very important events in my personal and family life, so will now make amends. After we got married, Marion and I lived for a while in Caerdydd before moving to the upstairs flat in my Aunty Enid's house in Penarth. Enid was for many years a teacher in the dockland area – where her star pupil was Shirley Bassey – before she became the first head of Caerdydd's first Welsh-medium primary, Bryn Taf. Her husband was a republican left-wing pacifist barrister, Ithel Davies, who had been imprisoned for long periods during the First World War as a conscientious objector, and subjected to considerable mistreatment. Ithel was still a committed nationalist but would have no truck with Plaid Cymru, while Enid, as befitting the daughter of one of the founder-members, was a faithful servant of the local Plaid branch. With such august landlords, it sounds fitting that it was from their flat in stately Penarth that I was taken one morning in a Black Maria to Cardiff Prison to spend time at Her Majesty's pleasure.

The imprisonment arose from the non-payment of a fine following the road-sign painting campaign. On the day the campaign was launched (at the home of Bishop William Morgan, translator of the Bible into Welsh), both Marion and I painted over some signs in Betws-y-Coed, and were duly fined. Weeks later, back home in Penarth, our first walk out with new baby Llion in his pram was to the local police station to pay Marion's fine, which left me to be sentenced to a month's jail by Penarth Magistrates. So I knew it was coming, and we had time to prime the press and prepare a few interviews and press releases beforehand. But seeing the Black Maria pulling up outside the flat was still a bit of a shock, and off I went, after saying my goodbyes. To be fair to the police, they handled me with care, and did not 'throw me in the back', as is usually their custom, but invited me to sit with the driver in the front seat, to enjoy the view. Such is Welsh justice!

People often ask me what it was like in prison, and I always start by saying that the point of the whole exercise is to rob the prisoner of his or her identity. However much we talk of rehabilitation and correction, as far as I can see, this basic fact has not changed. No doubt some prisons are better than others, and some categories of prisoners are treated more humanely than others, but in essence, the prison system treats you as a number, and not as a human being. I know there are no easy answers, but I am convinced that the prison system would be more effective if they treated all prisoners as human beings who can change for the better. I am also convinced of the fact that there are many, many people in prisons who should not be there at all.

But to come back to my own experience, the first thing that happens is that you are asked to strip, take a shower and are given a heap of clothes to wear. These clothes are called the 'prison uniform', and usually they don't fit, but you have to make do. In those days, you were also given a chamber pot to use as a toilet, and a plate with cutlery. It may be different by now, but using the pot and emptying it at preordained times was all part of the ritual to make you feel uncomfortable.

One of the first questions you get asked is, "How long you in for?" After hearing many of the newcomers mentioning fairly lengthy sentences, I ventured "Forty." "Forty months, or forty weeks?" came the reply. "Days," said I, feeling less than adequate in such august company. "What you in for?" they asked. "Non-payment of fines." "You didn't have any money, then?" And when I explained that I did have the money, but had decided not to pay so as to draw attention to the cause of the Welsh language, they were convinced that I was a bit mad; most threw a funny look at each other and never bothered me again on that subject. But one or two did ask me later to explain more about our campaign, and showed some real interest and a degree of sympathy as we got to know each other better.

The members of the so-called 'Free Wales Army' had been given a show trial in Swansea in 1969, and some of them were given fairly lengthy sentences on the very day Charles was invested as 'Prince of Wales'. Julian Cayo Evans, the leader of this intrepid band, was given a 15-month sentence, so he was still in Cardiff Prison when I arrived. Cayo was a colourful character and had the attributes of a natural leader of men, and during his stay in prison, he had become a firm favourite with the other inmates. If there was a matter they wanted to take to the Chief Warden, they would usually ask Cayo to be their spokesman.

He soon took on the role of being my unofficial guardian, and every day he would bring me a copy of the *Western Mail* so I could keep up with all the protests that were planned to coincide with my imprisonment. But getting the paper to me was no small matter! As we trudged round the exercise yard in threes every morning, Cayo would jump the lines one by one till he found me, and slipped me a copy of the coveted journal. This process was, of course, spotted quite regularly by the warder in charge. "If I catch you one more time, Evans 36412, you will be locked up for three days. Understand?" Cayo would say nothing, but one day as he approached the officer in question, he shouted, with his mischievous grin, "When we get a free Wales, you will be the first for the firing squad!" – to loud cheers from the ranks. It's fair to say that there was a degree of good humour around, especially when Cayo was involved. I will forever be grateful for his watching over me, and it was so sad when he died from diabetes in 1995, at a mere 57 years old. He was full of bravado, linked to a degree of showmanship, but he genuinely felt that Wales needed more of an edge to its public image. He was a character not to be forgotten.

Once you have been to prison for your cause, the rest of your life tends to be in the shadow of that experience. Whenever you face an injustice, you always say to yourself, "Should I not make a stand on this, and be prepared to face imprisonment if necessary?" At one time, our record company decided to withhold part of its corporation tax as a protest against the use being made of a portion of it to pay for nuclear arms. We were asking for assurance that all our taxes would be used for other purposes, as we did not believe we should be forced by law to pay for something we totally opposed. We were taken to court several times, had a polite hearing, and eventually had a half-hearted promise from the tax authorities that the portion spent on nuclear arms would be diverted to more constructive purposes. We knew that the promise did not amount to a cast-iron guarantee, and a part of me wanted to take the matter further, even to prison if necessary. But we let the matter go, and it has always been on my conscience that we bottled it.

The only other time, after the hot summers of the Sixties and Seventies, that I ended up in prison was for non-payment of my TV licence as part of the campaign for a Welsh language TV channel. After the early Cymdeithas campaigns to gain official recognition for the Welsh language on public signs, official forms, courts of law and the Post Office, we soon went on to the field of broadcasting, and it was becoming increasingly obvious that television was the crucial medium. Cymdeithas soon developed a policy of pushing for a channel dedicated to programmes in Cymraeg. And when the broadcasting authorities began planning a 'Fourth Channel' (prior to this we'd only had BBC1, BBC2 and ITV), this was obviously the chance to secure this fourth channel in Wales for Welsh-language programmes. It was a long and hard-fought campaign, and as it looked increasingly like ending in failure, many of us began refusing to pay for our TV licence, and the authorities took a hard line, knowing it could escalate to be a real problem for them. We were fined, of course, and the policy then was to refuse to pay the fine, and this usually meant a short prison sentence.

I was arrested at home in Waunfawr in August 1980 by two policemen who obviously weren't enjoying the experience. I knew one of them fairly well, and to be fair to them, they made the journey to HMP Walton in Liverpool as bearable as they could, and didn't handcuff me until we were entering the prison gates. On the way, they asked me if I wanted to stop for a coffee, and we did so in Queensferry. They took off their jackets so that we didn't look too conspicuously like two policemen and a prisoner, and had a welcome cuppa. I had been to Walton a few times on protest rallies when members of Cymdeithas had been inside, so when the policemen began to ask each other where exactly the prison was, I was only too pleased to be able to direct them! They left me at the prison, and I was given the usual treatment of an enforced shower and a pile of grey clothes, and shown to my cell. The animosity from the officers was evident, and the anti-Welsh comments flew. I realised anew that to be in prison in England for a 'Welsh' crime was not easily tolerated by the officials. But the thing I remember above all else about this episode is the book that lay on my bed in the cell. It was the story of Pasquale Paoli, the eighteenth-century Corsican leader. I read it avidly until lights-out, and carried on at the first light of dawn. A short break to empty my pot and queue for what passed for breakfast, and then back to my book. It all ended when the door was banged open and I received a shouted command to follow the screw to see the Chief Warden, and there was told that someone had anonymously paid my fine, so I was out. I protested, as I knew that I had a right to refuse to accept the offer (and really wanted to finish the fascinating story of Paoli), but I was given no choice, and was bundled to change my clothes and receive the train fare from Liverpool to Bangor.

The officer at the ironically named 'reception area' was a rather unsavoury character who made no secret of his hatred for Wales (and Ireland for that matter), and when he asked me the obligatory question, "Any complaints?",

I ventured to suggest that, as the prison was the main prison serving the north of Wales, they should have their signage in Welsh as well as English. He exploded, and shouted, "You do what you f***ing like in Wales, mate, but this is England, so f*** off back 'ome, and God 'elp you if you ever come in 'ere again!" I collected my train fare, and said to him as I left, with as much menace and false courage as I could muster, "Don't worry – I'll be back!" But I knew I had no intention of ever going back to his place again. And that was the last of my prison encounters.

I phoned home to tell Marion that I was on my way, and walked to Liverpool train station to catch the next train to Bangor. I walked a mile or so from Bangor station towards Caernarfon, as Marion had told me that she would be a bit late. It was great to see the children, and the first question they asked was whether I had received their letters. They were so disappointed when I explained to them that the prison would always keep letters for a few days before giving them to the prisoners, but that I would eventually get them sent on to me.

When I did receive them, they brought a tear to my eye. They were written in Welsh, of course, so I will translate them.

Llion Tegai (10 years old):
After midday on Wednesday, the phone rang all day. Your name was on every Welsh news bulletin after midday. Ray Gravell phoned as well, asking how we were, and asking for the address of the prison. You are bound to get a letter from him. Prison must be a depressing place, so I'm sending you this crossword, and the clues. Perhaps some

of them will be too easy for you, but also you can read the piece about biking on the back of the crossword. Perhaps you won't be able to recognise the *Sbio'n Gam* puzzle. You can write the answers on the back of this letter. I'll see you on Wednesday.

Cofion, Llion.

Elliw Haf (9 years old):
The weather is fine here today, and Mam is going to have her stitches taken out. We will go shopping today also. We went to Nain's house last night, and they had heard on the radio that you were in prison. We haven't eaten the fudge yet, but I think Telor has eaten a little piece! I will be looking forward to seeing you again.

Cofion cynnes, Elliw Haf.

Telor Hedd (7 years old):
How are things in prison? I have heard that the police can be a bit rough. How is the weather there? Perhaps we will go to the beach today. Remember, don't pay the fine or you won't get the Channel. I still look at the poster, 'No Channel, No Licence'.

Cofion, Telor.

There is a poignant sequel to Llion's letter. After my great friend Ray Gravell's untimely death, his wife Mari told me that he'd warned her that there was something she should never disclose until after he'd gone. And that was the fact that my imprisonment had such an impact on him that he couldn't bear the thought of me being in prison, and my wife and children at home without me. So he'd decided to pay my fine, and he was on the phone for hours, asking how this could be done, and managed to get the money sent to Walton. And that's how I came to be released against my wishes! It's so typical of Ray, a man who always wore his heart on his sleeve. How I wish I could have thanked him, and put his mind at ease that I didn't really mind at all. Dear, passionate Ray Gravell – a Welshman like no other.

But having left Walton, I only had a few hours at home with the family before leaving for the Dyffryn Lliw National Eisteddfod. I had to help prepare the Cymdeithas Tai Gwynedd stand, and attend a meeting of the Welsh TV Channel Working Group at Plaid's Summer School. Gwynfor Evans had intended leaving his role as Plaid President when he began his hunger strike in protest at the Thatcher government's reneging on their electoral promise to provide a Welsh-language channel, but he was persuaded to stay on, and this led to a vote for a Vice-President. Several names came forward, but many withdrew, which made it a race between Dafydd Elis-Thomas and myself, which Dafydd El won.

In the meantime, the Channel campaign was intensifying, with many protests, each one fiercer than the last, and the welcome given to Gwynfor in a series of meetings throughout Wales intensifying in passion with each one. A crucial deputation to the government was made by Cledwyn Hughes, Goronwy Daniel and the Archbishop of Wales, G O Williams. And suddenly, with no warning, the inconceivable happened – Maggie Thatcher was for turning after all! The decision to grant a channel for Welsh-language TV programmes was a great victory for the national cause, and one which would have a massive influence on Wales in cultural, linguistic and economic terms for years to come.

As for Sain, by the early 1980s, we had outgrown Gwernafalau, and we opened a new 24-track studio a mile down the road, on the site of old RAF huts used to store animal foodstuff. The 1980s, like the 1970s, was a period of intense, almost round-the-clock recording, and the releases of that period are still seen as the foundation of today's dynamic contemporary Welsh-language recording scene. And it was not only rock 'n' roll – it was everything from country and western to opera, traditional and modern folk music, and choirs by the ton! Geraint Jarman and Mike Stevens did their best work at Stiwdio Sain, and Aled Jones, Bryn Terfel, Bryn Fôn, Cerys Matthews et al all tarried there awhile. Great times.

CHAPTER 4

Alcohol and Me

THE TITLE OF this chapter might come as a shock to some, who know me as a lay preacher son of a real preacher. However, this is not going to be a sensation-seeking confession, but rather a timid attempt to show how alcohol has played its part in the political and social revolution which has changed Wales over the last 50 years.

When I went to university in Aberystwyth in the summer of 1961, I was a confirmed teetotaller. I had never been inside a public house, and had never had an alcoholic drink in my life. I thought it was a thoroughly stupid thing to do to spend money on getting drunk, and it was not for me. I was quite adamant that I could go through life without the help of alcohol. But woe is me – it did not take long for my fellow lodgers to talk me into trying half a glass of lager shandy in the pub a short walk from our digs. They said it would do me no harm at all, and indeed suggested I might come to enjoy it, in the company of good friends. And so it came to pass, and the half of shandy soon became a cloudy concoction of brown ale and rough cider, which my friends said was the ideal drink for beginners. How naïve I was (or to put it another, kinder, way – how innocent!). I need not bore you with the inevitable outcome, but suffice it to say I was not feeling very well by the end of the night, and left my mark on many a dark alleyway in Aber before arriving back at my lodgings.

And so I became a drinker of alcohol. The late Dr Dafydd Alun Jones, who did some excellent pioneering work with ex-soldiers and others who suffered from post-traumatic stress (indeed, he was one of the first to recognise the condition as a disease), used to say that the Welsh were a nation of extremes in their relation to alcohol: "They are either TT or Ta-Ta" was his unique way of summing up our national condition. And Wales has seen the best and worst of the extremes, with fervent abstinence campaigns sweeping the country alternating with periods of widespread drunkenness. For some reason, we find it difficult to settle down in a sensible middle ground. We are either careering towards alcoholism or desperately running away from it. This is perhaps overstating the case somewhat, but it is a good place to start this bit of my story!

So my year at Aberystwyth began, and as I was already guaranteed a place in the Welsh School of Architecture in Caerdydd, I fear the year carried on in a similar vein, with my regular sampling of the delights of the town's innumerable pubs. But I'm glad to say that there were other things – far more important things – happening in Aberystwyth that year, for there was growing talk of a new and radical language campaign, and a growing feeling that Plaid Cymru was not able to change the fate of the Welsh language. As the year wore on, criticism of Plaid Cymru grew in strength, and the need for a new, more radical, body to campaign more directly for the official status of the language began to take shape. I for one did not see the need for the language campaign body as a sign of the failure of Plaid Cymru, for I believed we needed both, and a political party could not confine itself to one cause, crucial as that cause might be. I remained a member of Plaid while some others made a point of leaving. I have never liked this trait in the Welsh political character – the belief that you have to leave one thing to join another. This, I fear, is a real Welsh weakness, for it constantly undermines our ability as a nation to work cohesively. There is a term in Welsh referring to the habit of one chapel breaking off from another to create a new one – "capel split". There is an old joke which springs from the same root: if a bunch of Welsh people were stranded on a desert island, they would build three chapels, so they could pass two on their way to their chosen one!

The seeds of Cymdeithas yr Iaith Gymraeg (for this became the official title of the new campaigning body) had been sown in the 1950s by a couple who lived in Llangennech near Llanelli, Eileen and Trefor Beasley. Bailiffs took most of their belongings for non-payment of fines imposed on them when they refused to pay their rates until the council produced bills in Welsh. But the final piece of inspiration was Saunders Lewis' 1962 BBC Radio Lecture, '*Tynged yr Iaith*' (The Fate of the Language). Saunders Lewis is a towering figure in Welsh culture and politics – a dramatist, poet and literary critic revered for his learning in many fields, a resolute European and nationalist. His lecture sounded a stern warning that Welsh faced certain death unless a radical campaign was waged to reinstate it as Wales' premier language. Broadly translated, his central message was that "nothing less than a revolution will suffice". Cymdeithas was founded during Plaid Cymru's Summer School in Pontarddulais in August 1962, and I believe that it is fair to say that the politics of Cymru and the Welsh language was changed fundamentally because of it.

First of all, we must place the growth of the language movement, and indeed the upsurge in Welsh national feeling in general, in its historic context. It was after all the 1960s, and there was a general feeling, especially among young people, that we could change the world. We felt as Wordsworth did when he first heard of the French Revolution – "Bliss was it in that dawn to be alive, but to be young was very Heaven!" – and our part of the revolution was to achieve full nation status for Cymru/Wales, and full official status for Cymraeg, the Welsh language. We were aware of what was happening in other countries around the world, and many of us took part in demos against the Vietnam War and the apartheid regime in South Africa, and were supporters of Martin Luther King's campaign in America, but our particular battle was for our own nation's right to exist and survive as a fully-fledged modern nation. They were heady days: we were up for the fight, and we enjoyed ourselves. We took the campaign seriously, but did not take ourselves too seriously. We knew we had justice on our side, but that did not mean the British justice system was on our side, and if we decided to break the law during a campaign because all other avenues had been tried and had failed, we knew we would have to accept the inevitable consequences. And so began several decades of campaigning for the language that saw hundreds of people (yes, several hundred) imprisoned for their part in those campaigns.

There's one principle which has underpinned the language campaigns from the beginning, and that is non-violence. It is generally accepted that this was adopted from the example shown by Martin Luther King in the US, and way before then, the campaigning model set by Gandhi in India. This meant that no methods would be used in Cymdeithas campaigns that could endanger life, but they could involve the destruction of property in certain controlled circumstances. In over 60 years of continuous activity, Cymdeithas members have respected this principle without exception, and it may be justly claimed that it is one of the few movements of its kind created in the 1960s which is still active today. And although I have had my differences with Cymdeithas from time to time, Wales would be a very different, and much sadder, place today without its tenacious perseverance.

There's no doubt that the principle of non-violence arose to a great extent from the Christian upbringing of most of the original Cymdeithas members, and it is no accident that two of the most prominent and long-lasting members – Angharad Tomos and Ffred Ffransis – are very much practising believers. But there were aspects of the Welsh Nonconformist tradition which needed to be challenged, and one of them was the narrow definition of what is socially decent and respectable. For example, when I moved to Caerdydd to begin my journey into architecture, I met up with other Welsh-speakers in the university Welsh society, and when I suggested we could all go to a pub after the formal meeting, I was met with almost complete disapproval, and some downright hostility. Many of the members were obviously at the place I was when I first went to Aberystwyth, so I didn't labour the point, but gradually saw the attitudes changing during that first year.

I remember one evening going with a few like-minded friends to look for a pub we could adopt as a place where Welsh-speakers could congregate. The only places where that was possible in Caerdydd at the time were the chapels, and the Urdd centre in Canton; there were also a few societies based on your county of origin (like 'Cymdeithas Sir Gâr' – the Carmarthenshire Society), but they were pretty formal, rather stuffy affairs, and mainly for older people. So the hunt was on for a new Welsh-speaking home! We found The Moira, a smallish, homely pub in the Splott/Adamsdown area, and it soon became the place to go to, especially on a Sunday night, for a good old sing-song. The irony of it all was that the songs were mostly hymns! I remember one enterprising youngster – named Gruff Miles (a nephew, by the way, of the film actor Hugh Griffith) – embarking on a mission to reintroduce folk songs into Welsh pubs, with some success. The Moira soon became too small to cater for all the Sunday night singing drinkers, so off we went again to look for a new venue. And so it came about that The New Ely in Cathays was established as the pub for Welsh- speakers (and anyone else interested), and it grew into a famous part of the Caerdydd scene for three or four decades.

As The New Ely – and other similar pubs which appeared here and there throughout the city – developed and spread its wings, of course there were other significant developments taking place. The campaigns of Cymdeithas yr Iaith were continuing apace, and moving on from gaining official status for the language to the courts, education, television and radio, and housing. There were also campaigns arising from the public and not run by Cymdeithas. Chief among these were local campaigns for Welsh-medium schools (often led by non-Welsh-speaking parents who wanted their children to have the chance to learn the language they had been deprived of), and local Welsh-language newspapers (*papurau bro*). The 1970s saw the start of the *papur bro* for Caerdydd, *Y Dinesydd*, and one of the early columns which created something of a stir was '*Dyddiadur y Dyn Dwad*' (Diary of the Incomer). *Dyn dwad* is a Gwynedd term usually referring to incomers (English mostly) who don't speak Welsh, but in the Diary, the tables are turned and the Welsh speakers are the incomers. It was written by the talented novelist and satirist Dafydd Huws, and his Diary was roundly criticised by some of the older readers because of its colourful language, and the fact that it was largely based on the goings-on at The New Ely pub.

So here we have a microcosm of the Caerdydd Welsh-language scene in the last decades of the twentieth century: chapel versus pub, old versus young, and a new, dynamic, irreverent culture arising out of the starchy old traditional one. But central to it all was the language: surviving, and growing new wings.

The growth of Welsh-language music and entertainment went hand in hand with the expansion of Radio Cymru and S4C, and it led to a flourishing Welsh recording industry and the spread of shops throughout Wales selling Welsh-language records, books and merchandise. This expansion, however, has been halted by the digital revolution, which slowed record and CD sales almost to a stop, and caused most record labels to become part-time outfits. One casualty has been the curtailing of the recording of choirs, traditional folk singing and other 'non pop' music, and it's not clear how the engineers and producers of the future will be created. But on the other hand, the digital platforms have made the whole world accessible for Welsh music, and it's probably true that more people are listening to Welsh-language songs today than at any other period in our history. This fact first hit us when the Welsh-language band Alffa clocked up a million plays on Spotify for their single 'Gwenwyn' (Poison), and more recently the video of my performance of 'Yma o hyd' before the Austria match flew past the million mark on YouTube – and it's still going! Another positive development is the popularity outside Wales of artists who don't sing in English, like Adwaith and Gwenno. There is no doubting the fact that the Welsh language, in many ways, has broken the language barrier.

The expected growth in clubs where Welsh bands are performing regularly has been slow, but Clwb Ifor Bach in Caerdydd is now a highly respected venue for good live music – although economic factors mean that it cannot give as much priority to Welsh-language bands as it would like, and certainly not as much as the founders would have liked. Clwb Tanybont in Caernarfon was a good venue for many years in the Seventies and Eighties, and Clwb Triban likewise in Rhyl, but both have now closed. Clwb y Bont in Pontypridd is going strong, despite the constant threat from flooding, and Saith Seren in Wrecsam is a beacon of light in that city of hope. However, the most encouraging story regarding Welsh pubs is the increasing number of community pubs – that is, pubs bought by the community to save them from closing, and the great thing about these is not only that they are a great example of grassroots community endeavour, but that they become community hubs for far more than merely the drinking of alcohol. So the revolution continues!

As a singer, the relationship between alcohol and music is a difficult one. Alcohol can make or break a performance. When the going is good, and enough alcohol consumed to banish all nerves and inhibitions, but with the audience still in a state where they can appreciate the music, and even the words, there is nothing quite like it in the human experience! But when the alcohol consumed reaches the stage when the music becomes background noise and merely an excuse for a drunken bash, that's when performers feel that they're in the wrong job. Going back to what Dr Dafydd Alun Jones said about "TT or Ta Ta", I fear that most Welsh performers have had more than their share of the drunken bashes. I sometimes get the feeling that Welsh culture is still suffering from the constraints of the eisteddfodic tradition – the "Close the doors, take your seats and pray silence for the next contestant" approach – and when those constraints are removed, all hell is let loose. Combine that with the thrill of breaking free from the religious pressure of abstinence, and you have the perfect storm! That's why many of us performers appreciate the odd night where the audience is sober, and sitting in comfortable seats, and are there to listen and hopefully to enjoy. It can be more of an acid test for a performer, but very much more rewarding when it works.

I experienced at first hand the coming together of the old eisteddfodic and *Noson Lawen* (literally 'Merry Night – a night of informal entertainment, usually a kind of local talent show) tradition and the new era of rock 'n' roll. It happened during the late 1960s (ah, that decade again!) when Robat Gruffudd, the founder of Y Lolfa (publishers of this book), invited the pioneering Welsh-language band Y Blew to perform in the village hall in Talybont, Ceredigion. With the band, to provide some cultural balance, was myself and the raconteur extraordinaire Eirwyn Pont Shan, with his unique mix of ribald verses and political anecdotes. I was the last to go on stage, and by that time, most of the audience – more used to seeing a local amateur drama performance or semi-classical concert – had gone, unable to withstand the high-decibel loudspeakers and risqué jokes. It was a brave cultural experiment and an unmitigated disaster, but Robat thought it was a great success. And it felt to me like we were at a significant watershed, and ever since, the two cultures have been kept apart – except for one notable exception when the band Edward H. Dafis made their first appearance at a *Noson Lawen* at Corwen Pavilion in 1973, and the two cultures met in a memorable night of singing and mirth (an event organised by Cymdeithas yr Iaith and recorded by Sain, and released as an album entitled *Tafodau Tân!*).

Another concert in the old pavilion in Corwen in 1988 marked my first quarter of a century as a singer, and it also marked the first mention of retiring! I thought it would be a good point to stop, and take another direction. I had already stood in a few elections, for Westminster in Ynys Môn and Conwy, and for the European Parliament for the North of Wales, though to no avail – I think the electorate knew better than me that I was not really cut out for the job. There was also the death of my father in 1984, and the desperately miserable process of divorce, leaving my home and buying a smaller house in Caernarfon where the children and I could meet. That was a real low point in my life, as anyone who has experienced a divorce will know, and to this day I do not fully understand what went wrong, except to say that if you want to avoid a divorce, keep clear of politics, stay away from radical campaigns, and avoid the entertainment industry at all costs. Our marriage didn't stand a chance, come to think of it now, and that's the only time in my life I had to cancel all my preaching engagements. Who was I to preach to others if I couldn't hold my own family together?

But I met Bethan in the little chapel in Garnfadryn on the Llŷn Peninsula when I resumed my preaching duties, and I was in love again, and things were looking up. So by the time the concert came around in July of 1988, I was actually thinking less of retiring and more of a new beginning with a band of my own, and the one we put together for that night was the basis of the band which has accompanied me ever since. I enjoyed having instrumentalists around me – far better musicians than myself – who, just as the folk group Ar Log had done in the early 1980s, gave new life to some of the old songs and inspired new ones, and Dafydd Iwan a'r Band was born.

Bethan and I were married in Garnfadryn on 24 September 1988. There was no alcohol at the reception, because Bethan's Anti Maira would not countenance it. Anti Maira was in many ways the heart and soul of Garnfadryn. She kept the village shop – which sold everything – she looked after the chapel, she booked the preachers, and she looked after the keys of the summer cottages dotted around the area when the owners were away. There were two things Anti Maira was absolutely firm about – one was that she was a firm supporter of the Royal Family, and the other was that there was to be no alcohol in the house. So I knew my place!

In fact, Bethan told me once that the first time she heard Anti Maira mention my name was on Investiture Day in 1969: as she settled down to watch the ceremony on TV, she said, "I hope that Dafydd Iwan doesn't do anything silly today!" But she was the one who booked me to preach in the little chapel, and she was the one who arranged the traditional tea (with cakes and trifle) for Bethan and me after the service. And so I fell in love, head over heels, over the peaches and cream. Anti Maira really was one in a million, and fed anyone who called by, without fail, in summer or winter. Despite her strong religious beliefs – or more likely because of them

– she always looked on the bright side, and always found reasons to smile in adversity. But we never discussed alcohol or the Royal Family.

Bethan and I settled in our present home in Rhos-bach after the wedding, within sight of Caernarfon Castle, but far enough from the town to make us believe we're in the countryside. To the west of us are the Eifl mountains on Llŷn, to the south the mountains of Eryri and to the north the flatlands of Ynys Môn. From our home, I keep a hand in running Sain record company, Tai Gwynedd housing association, and various voluntary bodies; from here I went to meetings of Cyngor Gwynedd for 13 years, and Cyngor Cymuned Bontnewydd for 30 years, and from here I leave on Sundays for the chapels that are still meeting in Gwynedd, Ynys Môn and further afield. And from here, despite several attempts at retiring, I still travel to gigs large and small all over the place.

Looking back at my long years of singing, the 1990s stand out as a decade of great nights for me and the Band. This was the decade when we performed in the Young People's Village at the Royal Welsh Show on the Sunday evening. As the DJ played the popular hits of the day (from the English charts), we feared it would be difficult to get the attention of such a mixed crowd of Young Farmers from all parts of Wales. But we needn't have worried: they switched from English hits to Dafydd Iwan a'r Band without missing a beat, and we never failed to get them going every year. It was also the decade when the Cnapan Festival in Ceredigion reached its pinnacle, and I found myself each year closing proceedings with '*Yma o hyd*' and '*I'r gad*' in a large marquee packed with thousands of joyous people. The Cnapan had started in a smaller shed in the village of Ffostrasol, but as it grew in popularity, it moved to a field outside the village, and attracted bands from all the Celtic countries. It was there that I met and shared the stage with The Fureys from Ireland, and I remember Finbar, the eldest of the Furey brothers, telling me to be careful with the nationalist passion my songs stirred up, as he feared they could lead to the kind of extreme actions that were seen in Ireland. It's as if the Irish, having achieved independence, were somewhat afraid of the passions the Irish rebel songs had engendered in the past. What he didn't appreciate, I think, is the basically different cultures that had created the songs of the two countries, but I could see he was genuinely worried.

There is an Irish dimension to another of my great memories of the Nineties, as we performed one gig before and another after the Wales-Ireland rugby match in Dublin every two years during the decade. It was a simple operation, and worked a treat for many years: we sold the tickets from Sain beforehand, and so we took not only the band, the instruments and the PA system with us, but also the audience! The best years were when we performed in the old Wexford Inn. As the decade wore on, Ireland was swept along by the success of the Celtic Tiger economy – fuelled by European Union funds – and the Wexford was modernised, and its name changed to the Mean Fiddler. Somehow, it was never quite the same after that, and the last time we performed there, the bouncers collected tickets from the people queuing and resold them, so the place became overcrowded and the gig had to be curtailed. Old Ireland had certainly changed, and our biennial trip to Dublin came to a stop soon after that. But it was great fun while it lasted, and I'll never forget the face of an Irish colleague of ours who worked for RTÉ, as he looked around him at the Welsh revellers standing on the tables singing their hearts out, on the Sunday morning before we all ran for the ferry back to Wales. He had a look of utter incredulity in his eyes, and a lingering smile on his lips. Before we left the pub, while sweeping the broken glasses into a huge heap in the middle of the floor, the owner looked at the heap, and looked at us, and said, "You Welsh shure know how to enjoy yourselves!" We half expected him to say something about paying for the damage, but he reached for a cheque he had kept behind the bar, and handed back the £100 deposit we had sent him a month before. Ireland at its very best.

CHAPTER 5

The King and I

IF WE WERE all given a blank sheet of paper to devise a blueprint for the Wales of our dreams, how many of us would actually include the Royal Family in our plans? Very few, I venture to suggest. After all is said and done, it doesn't make any sense, does it? What makes more sense is having an elected president every five years, as they have in the Republic of Ireland. They've had some pretty good ones as first citizens, while we in Wales have had to make do with a very expensive, dysfunctional family which isn't even Welsh.

But such matters aren't simple, are they? When I came to write my first song, my first serious effort at expressing my innermost feelings about Wales, what was the first line I came up with? *"Rwy'n cofio Llywelyn, byddinoedd Glyndŵr"* (I remember Llywelyn and the armies of Glyndŵr) – and they weren't exactly democratically elected men of the people, were they? Well, Llywelyn wasn't, even if Owain Glyndŵr could claim to have been chosen by the people. Both were aristocrats, products of their age, but what cannot be denied is that the assassination of Llywelyn, the last native Prince of Wales, in 1282 was a massive blow to the national spirit of Wales, and carrying his head on a pike through the streets of London suggests that the English king knew that full well. More than a century later, the uprising of Owain Glyndŵr, with the wide support of many of the most learned people of his day, was the last valiant attempt to create an independent and united Cymru. Since his defeat in around 1413, followed by a generation of bitter mourning and capitulation, the history of Wales has been a long series of campaigns against oppressive landlords, greedy landowners, and ruthless employers.

To name but a few: in 1839, workers in a wool factory in Llanidloes in Montgomeryshire staged what is now seen as the first action in the fight of the Chartists for democratic rights, and one of the first political actions by workers anywhere in the world, which led to a bloody confrontation with the military in Newport, Monmouthshire later that year. And in the same year of 1839, similar discontent amongst the working class led to the 'Rebecca Riots' in south-west Wales, where several tollgates – the charges at which had increased despite poor harvests and dire poverty in the agricultural community – were destroyed by men dressed in women's clothing. The 'Tithe War' of 1887 showed that it was the Welsh who were prepared to lead the fight against the Church's insistence on receiving a tenth of the land's produce, even when a parishioner was a Nonconformist. This radical theme continued as the unions led the fight for fairer conditions for slate quarrymen and coalminers, and in the more recent language campaigns, royal dissent and independence rallies – our story is one of constant radical opposition to exploitation and Anglicisation.

When non-historians like myself look to history, we all tend to pick out the bits that suit our narrative. So what better place to start than with Llywelyn and Glyndŵr? But that does not make me a royalist!

Since my reluctant leading role in opposing the 1969 Investiture of Prince Charles, my relationship with the present monarch has been almost like a long-drawn-out game of hide-and-seek. There have been many attempts to draw me into his web! The Prince's Trust has been fairly active in Wales, and has held many a musical event at which I have occasionally been invited to sing, but I managed to be otherwise engaged. Don't get me wrong – these events were perfectly fine in themselves, but I knew if I took part in them, that would become the story, with some seeing it as a betrayal, and others as some kind of political U-turn, so I preferred to stay away.

Two of the most important establishments I have been honoured to have played some part in developing are Antur Waunfawr, the centre for adults with learning difficulties near Caernarfon, and the Language Centre at Nant Gwrtheyrn on the Llŷn Peninsula. Both of these ventures were inspired by a very special person with a vision – R Gwynn Davies in Waunfawr, and Dr Carl Clowes in the Nant – and they are among the best and most pioneering institutions of their kind in Wales. Of course, to get such places going, it needs a lot of input by volunteers and a lot of money, so when the Prince showed an interest, they could not turn a blind eye. But I began to fear that Charles was following me around, and I was not in either of the places to meet him when he called. Years later, when I was a Gwynedd councillor and leading the Planning and Economic Development portfolio, a message came to say that Charles would like to meet me to discuss ways he could help the situation in Gwynedd, especially regarding housing. Detailed arrangements were suggested so that we could speak on a train whilst it was in a siding, but once again I knew that my meeting him would become the story, rather than any plans to help the economy. So I sent my most trusted officer to the appointment. There were other occasions when he came to Caernarfon to meet the council, and I was conveniently employed elsewhere.

But in 2019, a TV production company asked me if I would do a programme looking back at the Investiture after 50 years. As I thought highly of the producer involved, I agreed and things were proceeding well, with many people giving interesting insights into their experiences of 1969. Then one day, while filming, the producer asked – out of the blue – if I would be willing to meet Charles if he was amenable to the idea. I was dumbfounded, and the producer said it was just an idea that had grown during the filming, but I was free to refuse, of course. I asked to be given time to think on it, not really believing that Charles would be willing to take part. I did think about it, long and hard, and quite honestly could not think of a good reason to refuse the offer (if indeed such an offer arose). Only a few years earlier the MP Jo Cox had been murdered in broad daylight by a right-wing extremist who disliked her work with immigrants, and politics in Britain generally was in a pretty dark place. It suddenly struck me that this could be my opportunity to show that you can be completely opposed politically to someone without actually hating that person. I truly believe that racism is basically a form of hatred, and hatred must be eradicated from our lives, and removed from public life. So I said yes! And when the producers of the programme approached the Prince's office, they swiftly agreed, subject to a successful preliminary meeting with his aide. And so it came about that little old Dafydd from Rhos-bach met the future King of England at his Welsh country farm in Myddfai, near Llandovery.

I'd stayed the night in Llandovery a few weeks previously when we were recording a radio programme about the early years of Sain, and had met some local farmers who had a choir practice in the hotel we were staying at. One of the farmers said he farmed the land next to the Prince's farm, which led to some ribbing from all sides, and this is typical of the attitude in Wales towards the Royal Family. Very rarely does one come across open hostility, but neither do people at large take the royals completely seriously. But what some of the locals did want to explain was that Charles had done a lot to help various local causes, was always present in church services when he was 'in residence', and had helped to expedite a planning application for the Myddfai community hall, to which he had generously contributed. As well he might.

Our meeting was scheduled for 4 p.m. on Monday, 1 July 2019 – exactly 50 years after the Investiture at Caernarfon in 1969, which I had so publicly opposed. To some hardline nationalists (a rare breed, who have never really taken to me), this meeting was the ultimate proof that I was a traitor to the cause of Wales, and social media gave them plenty of scope to broadcast the fact. But most nationalists were bemused, not to say amused! In any case, I was by now fully committed to the meeting, without really knowing what to expect. As we approached Llwynywermod (which is the name of the royal farm – and which, by the way, could be translated as 'Wormwood Scrubs'), the security helicopter was circling above and there were armed police at the entrance, where everyone had to show passports and was kept waiting for checks.

At the end of the drive, yet more police, and the odd security person appearing here and there. We were told to wait for the royal command. The filming crew had fitted me up with the usual radio mike, and it occurred to me, if the actual conversation was to be held in secret, that a radio mike concealed on my body would hardly be allowed. So I asked the crew to check, and yes, of course I was relieved of my microphone. But come to think of it, nobody checked if I had a phone on me, which could have been in recording mode, or anything more sinister. Obviously the royal security people trusted me! Eventually, Charles appeared at a door and welcomed me in Welsh: "*Croeso!*" (so his term at university in Aber was not all in vain), and "It's very good of you to see me." We went inside to a room which has been fitted like a mediæval hall, decorated with Welsh quilts and traditional tapestry, where the Prince held his Welsh concerts.

We sat in this rather large room, about ten yards apart, with his aide (Welsh poet Grahame Davies) in attendance, taking notes. It was all pretty informal, and we talked a lot about interests we have in common

– the language, of course, traditional music and crafts, architecture and design, and the natural environment. He talked a lot about the work being done by the Prince's Trust and other projects he'd initiated, like the stately home in Scotland transformed into a training school for traditional building crafts and traditional music making. He studiously avoided any mention of the Investiture, but we did get round to politics, and I laid before him my vision of a Britain of independent self-governing nations and a devolved England working together for the common good, each nation free to contribute in its own way. His response was that he wished to truly understand the political temperature in each part of Britain, and pointed out that he was meeting the leaders of Sinn Fein in Northern Ireland the following week. The hour allocated to our meeting flew by, and I found my long-time adversary very easy to talk to, but my abiding impression as I left was of a man full of good intentions, but locked into a system he cannot control. He is a prisoner of an Establishment which he will find very difficult to change, even if he's inclined to. As if to illustrate the fact, his aide led me out through a room where a meeting was taking place – as we entered, everyone stared at us and one of them said, in a few stern words, that we couldn't go through that room, so the aide had to retrace our steps and swiftly show me out through the adjoining barn. So my royal assent was over!

I'll end this royal chapter on a more sinister note, for every post-Imperial power still depends heavily on massive security services. But as their empire slowly disintegrates, these special forces tend to create their own targets, and use unnecessarily heavy-handed methods to carry out their surveillance. Sometimes this leads to farcical situations, as witnessed in 1982 when a resident of Talysarn in the Nantlle Valley in Gwynedd saw someone placing something in the telephone kiosk outside his house. When the man left, the alert resident went out to see what was afoot, and found a rather sophisticated listening device stuck in a corner of the kiosk. The second-home-burning campaign was at its height, and the rumour was that one of the possible culprits lived in Talysarn. Nobody owned up to the bugging incident, and nobody was charged for the actual arson campaign. But there is no doubting the fact that the years between the mid Sixties and the mid Eighties saw a large number of undercover agents and *agents provocateurs* operating in Wales, purporting to fan the fires of nationalism with the aim of arresting the worst of the supposed terrorists.

In 1969, when the passions surrounding the impending Investiture were at their height, I experienced at first hand a rather pathetic attempt by an *agent provocateur* to put me in a great deal of trouble. I arrived at a concert in Llanrwst to find the place crawling with police, and two of them approached me to say they'd received intelligence that someone was out to kill me, so they were there in numbers to give me protection. I was ushered into the marquee where the concert was to take place, and shown into a small room in a corner of the tent. "We will be outside if you need us," they told me. As I sat there, trying to come to terms with what I'd just heard, and getting the guitar ready for the stage, a man came in, looking like a character from a B movie, and said in a hushed voice that we'd met previously at a Plaid do in Holyhead (I'd never seen him before, and never saw him again). He said that he had very little time, so he wanted to come straight to the point – I'll paraphrase concisely what he told me 54 years ago in a tent in Llanrwst: "We have a plan to assassinate the Prince, and you are the very man to help us." I didn't let him finish his sentence but told him to get out as quickly as his feet could take him, and added that I didn't ever want to see him again. When I got on to the stage five minutes later, I can assure you that I was in no mood to sing, but I did.

The highly charged atmosphere of the 1969 Investiture has long since dissipated, and Wales has settled back into its default position of being neither passionately for nor against the Royal Family. But there is a growing sense amongst the younger generation that the Royal Family is becoming more and more irrelevant, especially as the cost of living and housing crises worsen, and young people are increasingly worried about their future wellbeing. I don't have a hotline to the new King, but I cannot but wonder what's lurking in the back of his mind. Surely he knows that the shape and scale of the Royal Establishment has to be looked at, and eventually downgraded to a reasonable size. It was a great disappointment that he rushed to declare his eldest son the 'Prince of Wales', as he knows as well as anyone that Edward I used this title to endow his son with great wealth and power, and to incorporate Wales into the realm of England after the murder of Llywelyn.

In 2023, the priority for us now is to sort out the governance of Wales, and to ensure that the Senedd has full powers to organise Wales to the advantage of its people, and to decide on our own priorities. After independence, the people of Cymru will be able to decide what role, if any, they want the Royal Family to play; personally, I want Wales to be a free democratic republic with an elected President. And a great first step as we face our future would be for the Crown to return to the people of Wales its vast properties, including our rich coastal regions and the castles built by Edward to keep us in our place.

CHAPTER 6

'Yma o hyd' and the football connection

IF YOU'D LIKE to understand what we've all been singing for the past couple of years, here are the lyrics of 'Yma o hyd', followed by a rough translation into English:

Yma o hyd
Dwyt ti'm yn cofio Macsen,
Does neb yn ei nabod o,
Mae mil a chwe chant o flynyddoedd
Yn amser rhy hir i'r co';
Ond aeth Magnus Maximus o Gymru
Yn y flwyddyn tri chant wyth tri
A'n gadael yn genedl gyfan,
A heddiw – wele ni!

> CHORUS
> *Ryn ni yma o hyd! Ryn ni yma o hyd!*
> *Er gwaetha pawb a phopeth*
> *Er gwaetha pawb a phopeth*
> *Er gwaetha pawb a phopeth*
> *Ryn ni yma o hyd! Ryn ni yma o hyd!*
> *Er gwaetha pawb a phopeth*
> *Er gwaetha pawb a phopeth*
> *Er gwaetha pawb a phopeth*
> *Ryn ni yma o hyd!*

Chwythed y gwynt o'r Dwyrain,
Rhued y storm o'r môr,
Hollted y mellt yr wybren
A gwaedded y daran encôr;
Llifed dagrau'r gwangalon
A llyfed y taeog y llawr,
Er dued y fagddu o'n cwmpas
Ry'n ni'n barod am doriad y wawr!

CHORUS

Cofiwn i Facsen Wledig
Adael ein gwlad yn un darn,
A bloeddiwn gerbron y gwledydd:
'Mi fyddwn yma tan Ddydd y Farn!'
Er gwaetha pob Dic Siôn Dafydd,
Er gwaetha'r hen Fagi a'i chriw,
Byddwn yma hyd ddiwedd amser
A bydd yr iaith Gymraeg yn fyw!

CHORUS

Here Still
You don't remember Macsen?
Who was he, you don't know?
One thousand six hundred years
Is far, far too long ago.
When Maximus left our country,
Three eighty-three was the year,
He left us as a nation unbroken
And today – we are still here.

CHORUS
We're still here today! We're still here today!

Despite everything and everyone,
Despite everything and everyone,
Despite everything and everyone
We're still here today! We're still here today!
Despite everything and everyone,
Despite everything and everyone,
Despite everything and everyone
We're still here today!

Let the wind blow cold from the east,
Let the storm from the ocean roar,
Let the sky be split with lightning
Let thunderbolts shout their encore.
Let the fainthearted keep on wailing
Let the serfs all grovel and fawn,
In spite of the darkness around us
We're ready to greet a new dawn.

CHORUS

Remember that old Prince Macsen
He left our country as one,
Let's shout out to all the nations:
'We'll be here until Kingdom come!'
Despite all the furtive connivers,
Despite England's might, we're alive,
We'll be here for ever and ever,
The Welsh language will forever survive!

CHORUS

I don't usually remember the circumstances surrounding the composing of most of my songs. They just seemed to materialise, sometimes after lingering for some time in my head, and at other times as fast as I could write them down. Often they were written for a specific occasion – a concert or *Noson Lawen*, a TV programme, or language rally – and often the occasion itself suggested the message of the song. Usually I began with the chorus, or just the 'hook line', which often became the title, and then the words followed after the structure of the verses had been decided. More often than not, the chorus set the nature of the tune, and then the words and melody grew together, while I strummed the chords on the guitar. I'm the first to admit that my method isn't very sophisticated, and my tunes were limited by my fairly rudimentary skills on the guitar, but essentially I believe the strength of a song is based on the words, and the way the words and melody work together. When a song is more or less 'finished', that first time I sing it is the acid test – and sometimes I can tell immediately if it works or not. Very often, with the best ones, the first rendition brings tears to my eyes, and you can't argue with that!

With '*Yma o hyd*', I knew immediately that the song had something special about it. Ar Log were already at the Sain studios preparing for our impending tour of Wales, and the album to follow, and I raced to let them hear my new song. They liked it, and proceeded to arrange it for recording, slowing it to a more anthemic tempo in the process. We worked hard on the recording, and Dafydd Roberts added as many instruments as he could muster to give it as 'big' a sound as possible. The outcome is the version which has now been heard all over the world.

It's impossible to separate this song from the circumstances surrounding its birth. For a start, my wife and I were going through the first pangs of divorce, and as anyone who has experienced that hell knows, it isn't a good place. There's no point in my blaming anything or anybody from this distance, but suffice it to say that Marion had decided we couldn't continue as we were, with my travelling continuously in pursuit of my various interests and campaigns making her life difficult. I continued to believe that we could work things out, but Marion had made her mind up, and there followed an extended period of living apart in the same house, before the dreaded divorce papers came by post. I eventually left to live in a house in Caernarfon, near my children's school, so that we could keep in close contact. It was during the strange and sad period before I actually left that I sat one day in the attic of our house in Waunfawr to write the song that's now known as '*Yma o hyd*'.

In 1983, we were four years into the reign of Margaret Thatcher, the 'Iron Lady' who was hell-bent on changing the face of Britain forever. She wasn't remotely interested in Wales, but her plans led to the destruction of many of our communities, especially the close-knit communities which had grown around our coal mines. Even if we accept that coal mining was an industry which had to be closed down eventually for the sake of the environment, it was essential that this was done gradually, allowing time to develop new skills and new industries so as to avoid the destruction of these close-knit communities. But the coal industry was far too entwined with the trade union movement in Thatcher's eyes, and it had to be destroyed as part of her war against the unions. And Welsh communities bore the brunt, along with other similar communities in the north of England. The steel industry was also under threat, and factories were closed and asset-stripped in many parts of Wales, and the farming community was also threatened, leading to an extraordinary period where coal miners and farmers stood shoulder to shoulder on picket lines.

The defeat of the first devolution referendum in 1979 was another great blow to those of us who wished to see Wales gain more control of her own destiny, and its aftermath compounded the devastation caused by Thatcherite policies. There was a growing sense of despondency in Wales, and this was reflected even in the songs composed here at the time. My tour of concerts with Ar Log in 1982 was largely planned to counteract this feeling of dejection, although ironically it was called *Taith 700* (Tour 700), to mark the 700th anniversary of the murder of Llywelyn, the last native Prince of Wales. The tone and atmosphere of the tour, however, was one of defiant optimism, and the gigs were received with great enthusiasm. The main song I composed for the tour was '*Cerddwn ymlaen*' (We shall walk on), and it was the headline track of the LP released after the tour. The success of *Taith 700* led to another tour in 1983, and as we searched for a peg to hang it on, I remembered something Gwynfor Evans had once said: that he considered 383 to be the year when Wales started on its journey to be a free nation, being the year when the last Roman leader in Britain, Magnus Maximus, left these shores. That gave me the idea for the song – the last of the invading Romans left us exactly 1,600 years ago, and we are still here! Macsen was the Welsh name of Magnus Maximus, and we called the 1983 tour *Taith*

Macsen. 'Yma o hyd' began its journey to worldwide fame, and Macsen began to be a popular name for many Welsh boys born thereafter.

Many people regard 'Yma o hyd' as a political song, but in some ways it's the least political of my patriotic songs, because it's basically a celebration of our resilience as a nation, pure and simple. Many other songs – like its predecessor 'Cerddwn ymlaen' – have more political content, and more historical references, but 'Yma o hyd''s strength, I suppose, is its simplicity of message, and that the message of survival against all odds can strike a chord with so many different people and groups. The excellent video made by Siôn Llwyd for S4C to accompany the song before the World Cup gave it more political clout, and made a lasting impression, but it merely shows how the history of Wales – right up to the Miners' Strike of 1984–85 and the language campaigns of the last 60 years – is a story of continuous struggles by the working class of Wales for their rights against insensitive governments and oppressive industry masters and landlords. The simple strength of its message has lent itself to many different uses over the past 40 years – in 1986, for instance, I wrote new verses to support the striking quarrymen of Blaenau Ffestiniog, and later in support of the long dispute by the workers of Friction Dynamics near Caernarfon, which lasted for two and a half years, ending in 2008.

Over the years, many sports clubs have adopted the song as their own. Scarlets rugby (and Llanelli before that) were the first front-line sports team to use it as one of their signature tunes, and it's still played at Parc y

Me at Ysgol Gynradd Brynaman, aged about 5.
© Dafydd Iwan

Aged about 6, feeding a lamb on the farm near Aberhosan, Machynlleth, where we used to spend every holiday.
© Dafydd Iwan

My parents, Elizabeth Jane and Gerallt Jones.
© Dafydd Iwan

The whole family. L–R: Mam, Huw Ceredig, Alun Ffred (kneeling), Dad, Arthur Morus and me, with the chair Dad won at the Powys Eisteddfod.
© Dafydd Iwan

Singing at a Plaid Cymru fundraiser in 1968.

With fellow speakers Gareth Miles and Dr R Tudur Jones at the start of Cymdeithas yr Iaith's road-sign-painting campaign in 1969.
© with permission of the National Library of Wales

About to join the Gorsedd of Bards at the Bangor National Eisteddfod in 1971.
© with permission of the National Library of Wales

'Homes for Welsh people, not second homes': Campaigning in 1972 on something which is still a huge issue today.

With Elliw Haf, Llion Tegai, Marion and Telor in 1974.
© Dafydd Iwan

Reading my uncle John Tydu Jones' words over the entrance to the Memorial Chamber of the Canadian Parliament in 1979.
© Siân Thomas

With Gwynfor Evans in Sophia Gardens, Caerdydd in 1980, at a huge rally to protest the Thatcher government reneging on their promise of a Welsh-language TV channel.
© Marian Delyth

Addressing the rally, with Dafydd Elis-Thomas and Dafydd Wigley.
© Marian Delyth

With the Management Committee of Cymdeithas Tai Gwynedd in 1981. L–R: Bob Roberts, Dr Bruce Griffiths, John Gwynedd, Queenie Richards, Elwyn Gruffudd and Edwin Pritchard.
© Dafydd Iwan

On tour with Ar Log in 1982. L–R: Dafydd Roberts, Gwyndaf Roberts, Geraint Glynne, Steffan Rees and Iolo Jones.

Llangefni artist Jac Jones designed many of Sain's best LP covers. This was his design for my LP *Gwinllan a Roddwyd* (1986).
© Sain

Singing at a Wales Anti-
Apartheid rally in Sophia
Gardens, Caerdydd in 1986.
© Marian Delyth

Aled Jones receiving his gold disc for the album
Ave Maria at Stiwdio Sain.
© Gerallt Llewelyn

With Caio and Celt near Pen-llyn, Llanberis – one of my favourite photos.
© Glyn Davies

Back among the road signs – this time putting them up! Launching the new brown signs in Gwynedd as a county councillor.

Being made an honorary Fellow of the University of Bangor in 1998, with Glamorgan batsman Matthew Maynard and Vice-Chancellor Roy Evans.
© Dafydd Iwan

On the set of a Christmas special, with Welsh rugby greats Delme Thomas, Derek Quinnell and Ray Gravell, and Caryl Parry Jones.
© Dafydd Iwan

Addressing the Plaid Cymru rally in Machynlleth to commemorate the 600th anniversary of Owain Glyndŵr's first Welsh Parliament in 1404.
© Marian Delyth

With Bethan, Jo (Telor's wife) and all five children after the TV show celebrating my 60th birthday.
© Dafydd Iwan

At Caernarfon Castle, presenting Bryn Terfel with his first Sain gold disc.
© Gerallt Llewelyn

Bethan and Elliw join me to celebrate my Fellowship of Caerdydd University.
© Dafydd Iwan

Singing in the rain at the Ukraine match.
© FAWales and John Smith

Together Stronger at the City Stadium, Caerdydd.
© FAWales and John Smith

With Conor Roberts after the
Ukraine victory.
© Dafydd Iwan

After the Ukraine match
with Ben Davies.
© Dafydd Iwan

Sharing the celebrations with Jules and Mike Peters of The Alarm.
© Dafydd Iwan

At Caerdydd Airport, all ready to leave for Doha.
© Marcus Lawry

Enjoying my prize for singing on board!
© Marcus Lawry

Empty shops, decorated for the World Cup.
© Dafydd Iwan

The Doha *suq*, where the nations came together.
© Marcus Lawry

A reminder of the ongoing tragedy of the Palestinian people – the banner reads: 'Palestinian football martyrs who could have been with us at World Cup 2022'.
© Marcus Lawry

Islamic opulence at the *suq*.
© Dafydd Iwan

Iran supporters campaigning before the Wales game.
© Dafydd Iwan

Côr Dyffryn Clwyd Choir with Bryn Williams, Ian Rush, Laura McAllister, Jess Fishlock and Colin Jackson at the Embassy.
© Marcus Lawry

With Ian Rush, Jess Fishlock and Laura McAllister at the British Embassy do.
© Marcus Lawry

The elevation of Joe Allen!
© Marcus Lawry

The Al Jazeera interview – so what is Wales?
© Marcus Lawry

A chance meeting with Wales rugby legend
Ken Owens and family after the England game.
© Marcus Lawry

The Welsh dragon flying high in Doha.
© Dafydd Iwan

Early morning gathering at the bucket hat.
© Dafydd Iwan

The impromptu early-morning singalong at the Corniche.
© Marcus Lawry

The Red Wall in Qatar.
© Dafydd Iwan

Receiving the Inspiration Award from Sage Todz.
© Welsh Music Prize | Gwobr Gerddoriaeth Gymreig

With Huw Stephens, Sian Eleri and Sage Todz after the Welsh Music Prize awards.
© Welsh Music Prize | Gwobr Gerddoriaeth Gymreig

Scarlets every time they score a try. It's been played for many years before Cardiff City home games, and I seem to remember James Dean Bradfield saying he first heard the song being played over the PA system there. I'm also very proud of the fact that Wrexham, the team which has helped to put Wales on the world stage, also play it before every home game. I suppose we all feel at some time or other that we've had a rough time and a raw deal, and when we come out on the other side and realise that we have made it through, then this song is what we need to celebrate our survival. Whatever reason people have, all I can do is thank everyone who's identified with the song for their support; and most important of all, if it's helped my non-Welsh speaking compatriots to feel more a part of this great little nation of ours, then my cup is full to the brim.

Ian Gwyn Hughes of the Football Association of Wales phoned me out of the blue early in 2022, asking whether I would care to sing before the game between Cymru and Austria. It came as a complete surprise, but not an unwelcome one, and I wanted to know more. "I'm asking," said Ian, "on behalf of the team, for they were agreed that they would like to hear you sing '*Yma o hyd*' to get them ready for the game." A few years before, my sons had been in Moldova seeing our boys winning well, and after the game they were in a club, where most of the Welsh team joined them. Caio phoned me and said, "*Wnei di ddim credu hyn, Dad* (You won't believe this, Dad)" – someone had put '*Yma o hyd*' on the PA system, and the team had joined in, and Caio held his phone up so I could hear them. So, yes, I was aware that the song was known to the team, and I'd heard that a few of the players used to listen to it before each game they played. "You think it would work, Ian?" I asked, as I still wasn't sure. "Yes, I'm certain it would," came the reply.

I was later introduced to Dave Driscoll, an entertainment agent from Abercynon who was in charge of the singing in Cardiff City Stadium, and he became my 'Yma o hyd' agent for the next year of my life. Dave was a man of great experience in managing large-scale gigs, but this was a new challenge, and he took to it with great enthusiasm and a lot of original thinking. A few years earlier, Dave had been one of the people responsible for letting the Cardiff City Stadium crowd sing 'Hen Wlad fy Nhadau' unaccompanied – after many years of trying various ways of getting the best out of the anthem (with guest soloists, choirs and brass bands), it was decided to strike the musical intro, and then leave the crowd to sing without any accompaniment. And how the Red Wall responded! The singing of the national anthem had never been better, and now there was no looking back.

In preparation for my performance, Dave decided to place microphones throughout the stadium to get the best possible recording of the crowd singing, and he made sure that I had the best possible monitors to hear the track and my own voice, because I'd had several unhappy experiences in various stadiums in the past when I couldn't hear the music, or where everything was badly out of sync. So when I walked on to that little platform at the foot of the Canton Stand, where the stalwarts of the Red Wall were sitting (or rather standing), Dave had made sure that everything was in order.

I launched into '*Yma o hyd*', still a bit apprehensive about the whole adventure. But then the Red Wall joined in, like a well-drilled choir, and nearly blew me off my feet. That moment will stay with me forever as one of the highlights of my whole life. To sing a song that means so much to me for almost 40 years in concert after concert, and then to hear 30,000 Welsh fans joining in with such passion and feeling of joyful support – what more could a man want? And what added extra meaning to the experience was knowing that it all sprang from genuine support, and indeed love, for Wales, from Welsh speakers and English speakers. In that glorious moment, Wales came together as one nation.

And due to Dave's careful placing of his hidden mikes, we had an excellent recording of the crowd singing – not only of '*Yma o hyd*', but also of '*Hen Wlad fy Nhadau*'. We could then mix the crowd recording with the original 1983 track and produce the result which became the official World Cup version of '*Yma o hyd*'. It is in many ways a historic recording: not only were two recordings made 39 years apart and mixed into one, but it was the first time a live multi-mike recording of a football crowd was mixed with an original studio recording to produce the final version. And since we included some the recordings made during both the Austria and the Ukraine games, as well as the voices of the Wales team, we could safely say that there were around 70,000 voices on that recording! If we didn't win the Cup, I think we can safely say that we won the battle of the anthems!

Thus began a whirlwind six months for me: those two games, and the videos produced to showcase my performances, made me more famous than I have ever been. I would like to take this opportunity to thank the FAW, S4C and Afanti for the TV programmes, and the videos which gave those performances such meaning and impact. I was particularly impressed with the video which combined archive football footage with historical footage of radical campaigns by coalminers, language activists, Tryweryn protestors and striking workers. I played little part in putting that video together, so it was Sion Llwyd and others who chose footage from the archives to convey, and strengthen, the song's message about the survival of Wales despite all odds. A few people (very few in fact) have suggested that this video was too political – "pure Nationalist propaganda," said one critic – but scrutiny will show that everything in that video is the truth: they are actual scenes from news coverage of Welsh people standing up for their rights. And that, after all, is the story of Wales. Our story is not the Kings and Queens of England, nor is it the conquests of the British Empire; our story is that of Welsh people – the *gwerin* – demanding their rights, and standing up for justice, sometimes in very challenging circumstances.

One consequence of this newfound 'fame' is that people have been asking about my story. I've been very impressed by the amount of interest shown by those who don't speak Welsh in the language campaigns, and in the fact that I – along with hundreds of others – have been to prison as part of the campaign to get official status for the Welsh language. This has been the crowning glory of the *'Yma o hyd'* saga for me – that so many Welsh people, and others from outside Wales, have been made aware of the true story of Welsh radicalism. And I feel that I am privileged to be able to go to schools and other places throughout Wales to tell this story, and to answer questions about it. Children especially want to know more – about what it was like to sing along with a full stadium of Red Wall supporters, about the inspiration for the song, and what it was like to be in prison. I'm also asked to give the background to the Tryweryn story, as I was living in the area at the time of the drowning of the valley, was in school with children from the drowned village, and my father marched with the residents to Liverpool.

This process of teaching the children of Wales their own story is fundamental, I believe, to true education – to help us understand where we have come from, and what's shaped the Wales of today. We mustn't dwell too long in the past, but we have to know where we've come from in order to be able to decide we're going, and the new Curriculum for Wales is an important step in this process.

The more immediate result of the '*Yma o hyd*' football connection, of course, was my meetings with both the men's and the women's national squads, getting to know the people driving the Football Association of Wales project, and the trip to Qatar. The thing that really impresses me about the way the FAW go about things is that they don't make a big song and dance about it, they just seem to make it happen as if it's the most natural thing in the world. So it was with meeting the teams. If they'd warned me days before, and told me I could say a few words to the whole squad, I'd probably have lost a few nights' sleep. But I was in the team hotel in the Vale one day, and one of the FAW personnel – I forget who – casually said, "Would you like to meet the squad?" I must have said yes, because the next thing I knew, a door opened and there they all were, having just finished their lunch, sitting around getting ready for the afternoon training. They all applauded when they saw me, and that was enough to take my breath away, then Ian said a few words of introduction, then turned to me and asked me if I'd like to address the squad.

I'm pretty good at impromptu speeches, having had plenty of practice in rallies, protests and courts of law. But this was impromptu with a difference, as I was speaking to a crowd of people who were heroes of mine, and people I hadn't ever expected to meet in person. I just hoped that what I said made some sense. I then had a chance to speak to many of the squad personally, and was impressed with their down-to-earth humility and how easy it was to talk to them. The only problem I had was trying to avoid repeating the obvious cliches! When I spoke to Joe Allen, I suddenly remembered hearing that he kept chickens, so I asked him in Welsh, *"Shw ma'r ieir?* (How are the chickens?)"*, and he answered with a smile, *"Maen nhw'n fyw* (They're alive)," as if it was the most natural question in the world. I had quite a long chat with some of the older players, like Hennessey and Gunter and Gareth Bale. Gareth exemplifies what's true of all truly great sportsmen and women – the greater they are, the easier it is to engage with them, and he has certainly been the prime statesman of Welsh football for a decade and more.

As the World Cup approached, Dave Driscoll organised many events for me. In addition to my usual gigs, there were requests from all quarters asking me to make an appearance, or to give interviews for TV, radio and the press. On 30 September 2022, the Band and I played to a full house in Theatr Soar in Merthyr, then went on to Caerdydd to sing as part of the YesCymru/All Under One Banner Independence rally, and back to Merthyr for another full house at Soar. We went to a nearby pub for a pint after the show, but when we then tried to get a taxi to the hotel, we found that Merthyr on a Saturday night isn't the easiest place in the world to find one. As we watched the traffic trickling by, a big spanking white police van came along, and the driver recognised me – "It's Dafydd Iwan!" the policeman shouted. Wyn Pearson, our lead guitarist, always one for an opportunity, shouted back at him, "Any chance of a lift to our hotel?" To our surprise, "Yes, why not? Jump in!" came the reply. And that's how the Band and I had a police escort to the Premier Inn in Merthyr! The young chap who was looking after the reception that night nearly fell off his stool when he saw a police van depositing his guests outside, but he recovered in time to take a photo of us all – for police records, I suppose!

Covid was still around, and people were still apprehensive about being in large gatherings, but there was a general spirit of getting on with things, and trying to get back to normality. A TV crew from the Gaelic TV service in Scotland came down for an interview in Welsh (to be voiced over in Gaelic), because they recognised the significance of having a song in a Celtic language as the official World Cup anthem. The following week, a leading French football magazine gave me a long interview, which led to an in-depth article about the relationship between the language and Welsh football.

During the next few days, I filmed a programme with Elin Fflur for S4C in the very successful *Sgwrs dan y Lloer* (A Conversation by Moonlight) series, filmed some more footage for the S4C video to accompany the song, recorded a radio programme with Huw Stephens about the albums of children songs I did with Edward back in the day, and visited the Welsh school attended by Dave Driscoll's children in Abercynon. Then at the weekend I sang in two prizegiving nights at the Coal Exchange, one for NHS workers and the other for the unsung heroes of local football teams. During this period, it was officially announced that '*Yma o hyd*' was the chosen anthem for the Wales team in Qatar, and I had two in-depth interviews with Don McRae of *The Guardian* and Dave Sheinin of *The Washington Post* (as Wales would be playing the USA in Doha).

Stuffed in between the football-related gigs, we went on a rather bizarre, but interesting, gig to Amsterdam from Hull. There were several Welsh bands and entertainers on the bill, and it was organised by the enterprising Elfyn Thomas. The noteworthy aspect about it was that the gigs happened on the ferry as we crossed over, and then as we crossed back. Amsterdam was merely the filling in the sandwich, but as luck would have it, we experienced one of the worst storms seen in the area on the way back, so staying on my stool was almost as difficult as keeping in tune. But a good time was had by all!

Back in Wales and on dry land, the CD of the new version of *'Yma o hyd'* was released on 7 November, and I spent the whole day doing the rounds of TV programmes and radio studios, and on the 10th I took part in a historic live TV broadcast which linked dozens of schools throughout Wales. It's reported that tens of thousands of Welsh schoolchildren joined in the singing of *'Yma o hyd'* on that day to celebrate the 100th anniversary of Urdd Gobaith Cymru, the Welsh youth movement. More school visits followed, and yet more interviews, and on Saturday, 18 November, I was invited to sing before Newport's game at Rodney Parade in Casnewydd. It was a glorious day, and the reception I got was very warm indeed. That evening I was one of the artists singing in a concert to coincide with switching on the city's Christmas lights, and once again the audience response was incredible. Not so long ago, Newport and Monmouthshire couldn't decide whether they were in Wales or not; by now, Casnewydd is most certainly a Welsh city to its very core. It was the ideal send-off before our flight to Qatar the following morning.

CHAPTER 7

Qatar

I MUST CONFESS from the start that I wasn't burning with enthusiasm to go to Qatar. The whole saga surrounding the decision to hold the World Cup finals there left a bad taste in the mouth, and the stories coming out of the country about the building of so many new arenas, and the deaths of so many of the workers drafted in to build them (although the actual figures remain unclear), made one wonder whether we should boycott the whole affair.

But all of us had known where the finals were going to be held, and it would have made more sense to boycott the whole competition rather than make a belated stand at the final hurdle. By then, the very prospect of seeing Wales taking part in such a worldwide event overcame all objections, and there was no way I could turn down the chance to be part of such an occasion. Indeed, as time wore on, and as TV programmes and press articles about Qatar appeared almost daily, it was clear that more was being heard in the rest of the world of the downside and less attractive features of Qatar than would have been the case had they not hosted the tournament. There was another factor which counted in Qatar's favour in my mind: one news channel I depend on to hear the other side of news stories from the Middle East is Al Jazeera, and I knew their headquarters were in Doha.

So it was that I found myself en route to Doha, flanked by Dave Driscoll and his business partner Marcus Lawry; not quite knowing what to expect, but ready for anything. It started in Caerdydd Airport, with fans wanting selfies and asking me to sign their bucket hats every step of the way. I've never been so relieved by a pass to the VIP lounge! Was I beginning to be a captive of privilege? I wondered – but no, I'd been warned that I'd be a target of constant attention, so a bit of peace and quiet was welcome. But that soon evaporated on the plane: I was called by the cabin crew to the bar and asked to sing '*Yma o hyd*' over the plane's public address system – a request any self-respecting singer would turn down without any hesitation. But we were on the way to the World Cup, and Wales were going to win, and there were family members of the team on the plane, and a loud demand for the song, and everyone was in good spirits... I spotted a bottle of Jack Daniels on the shelf, so I said, "If you give me a glass of Jack Daniels, I'll do it!" A glass was promptly placed before me, Dave held a phone playing the track on one side of the tiny mike, and I sang on the other side. It must have sounded terrible to the passengers, but the cabin crew seemed to be enjoying themselves, and I certainly enjoyed the Jack Daniels. And so began the Doha adventure!

We'd all seen footage of the impressive skyscrapers which have sprung up in Doha over the past 20 years, and were perhaps half expecting to be housed in one of them. But as it eventually turned out, we were put up in a pretty ordinary apartment building on the city's outskirts, surrounded by tired-looking shops and tiny cafés run by Asian incomers. The question we asked ourselves was: who lived in those apartments when there was no World Cup? The only possible answer was that they usually housed the Asian workers who had built the stadiums and who ran most of the country's services, but that they'd been moved out for the duration of the competition to make room for the likes of us. On our way to the stadium during our stay there, we saw mile after mile of half-built and unfinished houses, for Qatar is a country based on the labour of incomers, mostly from Asia, and they are obviously preparing to take in millions more in the coming years. Only around 12% of the population are native Qataris, and they for the most part are wealthy, and supported very well by the government. Everyone else has to work hard, but we heard very little complaining – "It's safe here," said one Syrian taxi driver, who also worked for a large company as his main job, "and if you are not a Qatari and prepared to work, you can have a good life."

Looking back at it all now, the Qatari adventure seems almost surreal. It's as if the Qatari government had built a gigantic film set to stage the finals of the World Cup, and to accommodate the thousands of football supporters from all corners of the earth. Work was barely finished on this lavish film set, with recently planted bushes and flowers wherever one looked, and fresh paving stones often coming to an abrupt end. The impressive collection of new skyscrapers in the wealthy centre of Doha seemed mostly empty, and away from the main shopping precinct, whole rows of new shops were boarded up, and the boards painted with the World Cup logo and dancing Qatari cartoon figures in white robes. The film set's centrepiece was the *suq* – the traditional market place of Middle Eastern countries, a place full of character and interesting artefacts, but again one suspected that it was not very old, and was an elaborate contribution to the Doha World Cup visitor experience. But ancient or not, sitting in the *suq* could be a memorable experience, as wave after wave of colourful, chanting football fans passed through in high spirits. And in the conspicuous absence of alcohol, this rowdy and joyful international pageant never displayed any unpleasantness or any signs of violence, even when two traditional football enemies came face to face. And that is the overwhelming memory of World Cup Doha – football fans from all corners of the world enjoying themselves in the unlikely surroundings of a Middle Eastern country most of us had never heard of before – an experience which will probably never again be repeated in a single city.

And what of the Welsh contribution to it all? The less said about the football, the better, perhaps, for we witnessed the tail end of a golden era in our national game. After the glorious experience of the Euros in 2016, we scraped through to the World Cup finals in two great matches in the Caerdydd City Stadium, and then it all came to a grinding halt in Doha. Our talisman Gareth Bale and many of his comrades showed signs of football fatigue – though I for one will never complain, because they had given us all many years of national pride and thrilling entertainment, and it was bound to end sooner or later. It's only sad that the end came in the World Cup, on the biggest stage of them all. But we got there, and the world came to know about us, and I'm so proud of the way the Red Wall stayed to the end of that third game and applauded Gareth and his team. The Welsh supporters, and the team itself, conducted themselves with dignity to the very end, in the face of extreme disappointment. And now we face a few years of building a new national team, and the future can be bright again, led by our brilliant fans and the resourceful and imaginative FAW.

But of course, the football was only peripheral! There were other things going on, and I was kept busy entertaining the troops between matches, with Dave and Marcus whisking me from one venue to another to do my bit. The most popular Welsh venue was the restaurant (with alcohol) run by Rhodri Ogwen Williams, and there was a veritable scrum of people queuing to get in whenever you went there. I succeeded in getting in on three occasions, and the welcome from Rhodri and his wife was second to none. The only problem was that I was hounded for selfies the moment people recognised me, until it became rather overwhelming. I learnt after the first visit that aiming for a corner seat with a pint and keeping my head down was my best plan. Having said that, the atmosphere was electric, especially as that first game approached, and Dave and Marcus made sure that my record was played at strategic times during my visit, and gave me a hand mike to sing along with it. Needless to say, the singing of the crowd was deafening, and made us feel the Cup was within reach! My best recollection of that great venue was the night when I was joined by three of my sons – Llion, Caio and Celt. And it was surprising the number of other people we knew who turned up there. It was like the Eisteddfod and the Royal Welsh rolled into one.

The most formal event I attended was the reception at the British Embassy. We almost didn't make it as we'd been told that we didn't need to show our passports, so we left them in the safety of the apartment. Of course, the first question asked by the security man at the entrance was where our passports were. We were kept waiting for half an hour while the security officers phoned around, and in the end, someone from the Embassy had to come out to verify that we were indeed official guests, and I was to perform. By the time we got in, the food was getting cold, and they were searching for me among the bushes. The people there were almost all from Wales, so what exactly the object of the exercise was isn't clear, but the food was Welsh lamb and all kinds of other Welsh delicacies (specially flown in for the occasion, I suppose). The Urdd Youth Choir from Clwyd were there to sing – and very good they were – and I was to join them for a couple of songs. It went very well, but once again, it was a Welsh performance for a Welsh audience, and its purpose was not clear. I had a word with a nice gentleman who had a smattering of Welsh, and he turned out to be the British Ambassador to Qatar, who had been born and raised on the Welsh border.

Two evening get-togethers were organised by Wonky Sheep, the company which specialises in football trips for Welsh supporters, and who had arranged the trip to Qatar for a large contingent of the Red Wall. These nights were billed as 'Legend Nights', where former football stars like Ian Rush, Danny Gabbidon and Jess Fishlock, alongside people like Laura McAllister and Women's coach Gemma Grainger, were interviewed by a host of Welsh TV and radio presenters, and people like me thrown in for good measure. They were held at the impressive Sheraton Hotel, one of the most prestigious hotels in Doha, in a vast beer garden, and they were very enjoyable events, despite the ridiculously expensive beer. Dave and Marcus helped with the technical arrangements, and Welsh DJs were there to play the background music, and yours truly with the obligatory *'Yma o hyd'* to bring things to a close. What I could not fathom was where all the artists who had been brought over by Wales Arts International, the Welsh Government and the Welsh Arts Council were. I still can't work out where they were performing, if they performed at all. These 'Legend' nights would have been ideal for them, and with a bit more joined-up planning between the various Welsh agencies involved, such events could have been even more memorable.

The other event organised for the Welsh supporters was an early-morning sing-song by the 'bucket hat' – which passed for the Welsh Pavilion, I suppose – next to the British Pavilion on the Corniche seafront. It was billed for 9.30 in the morning and, as all roads near the Corniche were closed to traffic, the taxis dropped us off some way from it, but we could see hordes of red T-shirts appearing on all sides, with no-one quite sure which route to take. Eventually, with that instinct which belongs to crowds, we all converged in one general direction, and soon saw a sizable gathering around the bucket hat.

Everyone was in high spirits, and there wasn't a cloud in the sky. There were impromptu songs by the supporters – some apparently composed for the occasion – and then the Urdd Youth Choir from Clwyd brought some more polished singing to the event, and after that I joined in with them in some songs. Largely due to its spontaneous and unrehearsed nature, this was probably the best event of the whole Qatari experience for us Welsh supporters, and it did have that air of genuine Welsh presence which we were all looking for. After it was all over, while the Red Wall lingered to extend the experience as long as possible, I had a long and interesting interview with a film crew from Al Jazeera TV, during which I had plenty of opportunity to explain what Wales is about, and how our language is different to English, and what taking part in the World Cup meant to us as a nation. All in all, a thoroughly worthwhile morning's work!

As Wales' three games were spaced over 10 days, we had plenty of time to have a wander around Doha. Not that there is an abundance of things to see, as Doha has virtually grown out of the sand in a short space of time, and there are no notable landmarks and certainly no ancient or historic buildings to see. But on one of the days I had to myself, I met my son Celt and his friends and we went to the impressive modern building which houses the Museum of Islamic Art. If ever you are in Doha, this is certainly worth a visit, if only to remind us of the rich and varied cultures of the world, way beyond our rather restricted world view. The lasting impression I was left with after a few hours in this Museum was that Islamic culture was well advanced long before ours in the West

– in printing and design, their work was very impressive in its variety and quality when we were struggling to get going. But the highlight of the visit for me was the more recent history of architecture in Iraq, and especially in Baghdad, under several leaders, including Saddam Hussein. They commissioned some of the world's best architects to design buildings for that city, including the renowned Welsh-American Frank Lloyd Wright. His design for Baghdad University was not built, but there was a full-blown model of his intended creation in the museum, as well as creations by architects such as Le Corbusier and Mies van der Rohe. As I looked at these impressive buildings, all I could think of was the speed with which we were drawn into that terrible bombing of such a great city, and such an ancient civilisation.

But to return to the football for a while, I remember feeling that there was something missing amongst the Welsh supporters before the Iran game. It was a very warm day, and we had to queue as always in the glaring sun. Perhaps that was part of the reason why our supporters seemed subdued. In contrast, the Iran supporters were in full voice, although much of it seemed to be in protest against their own government. There were several groups among them collecting names on a petition and distributing leaflets under the 'Woman-Life-Freedom' banner. God knows, they have plenty of cause to protest, and their football team joined in during their opening game, which put them at huge risk in such an authoritarian country. But their supporters obviously thought that the presence of the team in the World Cup was a great opportunity to make their voices heard, and raise awareness of their cause. Compared to them, Wales were quiet, and I was already beginning to feel that things were not going our way. Should we have organised a get-together for a song or two before that game? The conditions weren't ideal, as the concourse surrounding the new stadium was pretty devoid of atmosphere (as well as alcohol and food), but on reflection, we should have thought of something to help raise our spirits. However, it was what it was, and if the Red Wall felt deflated, the feeling perhaps spread to the team. And we were well beaten.

I do think we can all be extremely proud, however, of the team's achievement in getting to Wales' first World Cup since 1958, and in uniting Wales behind them, and of the Red Wall for acting as such excellent ambassadors of our little country on the world stage. Let's hope there will be many more successes in Wales' footballing future.

CHAPTER 8

A Welshman Abroad

THE FAME BUSINESS is a double-edged sword, and it can be soul-destroying. I hasten to add that I have only been subjected to fame in small doses, and that helps to keep your feet firmly on the ground. This is true of most Welsh-language artists – and those who ply their trade in other lesser-used languages throughout the world – you can become very famous among a limited number of people, and still live most of your life as an ordinary member of the public, without being recognised. Those artists who are constantly recognised, and even hounded by the press and photographers, have a choice, I suppose – either to lap it up and enjoy it while it lasts, or become hermits in constant flight from the paparazzi. But where it can become a real problem is when those who depend on a degree of publicity to further their public image begin to attack the press for invasion of privacy. It's a problem I'm thankful that I don't have to face, although I had a small taste of it during the lead-up to the football World Cup in Qatar. I admit that it was a rather strange, but not entirely unpleasant, experience to be stopped in a Caerdydd street during that period by someone asking, "Pardon me for interrupting, but are you that man who sings that song?"

That's called being famous for something, but it's not totally clear for what.

I was in America once, during the North American Festival of Wales (which used to be called the North American *Gymanfa Ganu* [a hymn-singing extravaganza] but is now more of a festival of all things Welsh-American), when a young girl asked me, "Are you famous?" She had obviously been sent around to get the autographs of 'famous people'. I've been to that Festival a few times, and always leave with mixed feelings. Unlike the Irish, the Welsh in America have almost been assimilated out of all recognition – until, that is, someone lights the Welsh fuse, and suddenly thousands of people of Welsh ancestry come out of the woodwork and assemble in one big *Cymanfa Ganu* where Welshcakes and lovespoons abound, before everyone disappears back into their American homes again. It's a strange gift the Welsh people abroad have of almost disappearing into the background, whilst our Irish cousins have made a point of asserting themselves as a permanent feature of the American scene, and their Irish pubs are popular gathering places throughout most of the world.

During all the years we at Sain have been selling Welsh recordings, we've tried our best to develop the North American market for our products, but not very successfully. We had some good outlets for a time, and did manage to sell a few, but once again found that the Welsh seemed to be invisible, while the Irish music market was always buoyant, and Irish bands – as well as Scottish groups – were constantly touring the US and Canada. I'm not exactly sure what the explanation is. It may have something to do with the language: because the Welsh language is far more prominent in our culture, especially our folk music, than the Irish language or Scots Gaelic, perhaps there has been this perception that Welsh songs are not so accessible. But I think the real reason has more to do with our national character, which means we are not as self-confident and as assertive as our Celtic cousins and other nationalities.

Yet this is certainly not true of those Welsh workers who left our coalmines, slate quarries and steelworks to look for work in America when things were opening up there. Because of our superior knowledge and experience in these industries, we found ourselves more often than not in the driving seat and running many of these industries, while the Irish and the Italians, for example, formed the workforce. As a result, the Welsh in many parts of the US had the reputation of being on the side of the owners rather than the unions, and I remember being reminded of this in a workers' club in downtown Pittsburg, where the audience were rather hostile, to say the least. I think I won them over in the end, but I remember having to sing every song I knew, almost as punishment for being Welsh! As some songs came round for the second time, I turned to Hefin Elis, who was accompanying me, and said, *"Gad ni drio 'Hen Wlad fy Nhadau'* (Let's try *'Hen Wlad fy Nhadau'* to see if that will work)!" And indeed it did! It was in that club that I was offered a smoke of some kind of drug, and when I said, "I don't do drugs," the girl almost fell off her chair, and shouted, "What? A folk singer going round the clubs and you don't do drugs? My God, what next?"

The United States is a vast country with vast problems and huge contradictions, and since the emergence of Donald Trump, it has fallen even further in my estimation. Of course, it's also a country of great talent and immense possibilities, but I fear the negatives outweigh the positives at the moment. When I went there first, soon after Wales' failed devolution referendum of 1979, Hefin and myself travelled from one city to the next by plane or bus, and stayed with families who had Welsh connections. The first house we stayed in was the home of a young university lecturer, and we arrived rather late while he was watching TV. He said a brief welcome and waved us towards the fridge: "The beers are over there." He had evidently been warned that these Welsh troubadours were big beer drinkers! We sat down to watch TV with him, and he briefly explained that the bad guys were over there, and the police were trying to get them. We watched in silence for ten minutes without knowing whether we were watching a film or a news broadcast, but it eventually dawned on us that it was an actual real-life case of hostage taking, and it went on for a very long time, with the lecturer transfixed. That experience has stayed with me ever since, and says a lot to me about the US of A – a country where the people are not quite sure of the dividing line between the real world and the world of make-believe. Only a country with such a mindset could create a monster like the Donald, and didn't Reagan once say that he knew the Holocaust had happened because he'd seen the film?

The question many Americans liked to ask their visitors was "What do you think of America, then?" Whatever answer one gave, they tended to say, "Don't generalise – the US of A is an enormous country," but they really gave the impression that they wanted you to praise the place and the people. Of course, they were right in the sense that it's truly a gigantic country, and full of mind-boggling variety and scenery and cultures. But I can't see myself ever going there again. The last time I was there has become a memory I would like to erase, for three days before the fall of the World Trade Centre towers, I was filming for an S4C programme of songs about America. There was one song, written probably towards the end of the nineteenth century, which was a kind of send-up of the fact that everything in America is big, bigger than everywhere else. We thought the top of the Trade Centre towers would be an ideal place to link into this song, and we arranged to go to the top. Unfortunately, that first visit proved to be a bit of a technical disaster because all the cables and aerials interfered with the sound. So we made another visit, and had to twist a few arms to get us to the top a second time, without a pre-booked appointment. Anyway we managed to wangle it, and this time the recorded sound was clear of interference and we got the links done. For some reason, the producer wasn't altogether happy with the link, so we did another one as a back-up in a waterside location, and then packed our things ready for the flight home.

I remember vividly being at Stiwdio Sain on our first day home, walking past the TV, and seeing the smoke billowing from the Twin Towers, where we'd been two days before. I stood transfixed, and thought of all the people who'd been so willing to help us during the filming, most of whom would now probably be dead. It was one of those tragedies in which we can all say where we were when we heard – or saw – the terrible news.

As I write this, the threat of international terrorism has been largely displaced by the very real and frightening threat of record high temperatures, and wildfires stretching from the Greek islands to North Africa, the United States and Canada. Suddenly, we are all being made cruelly aware that global warming is not a distant possibility, but an existential threat to us all. Perhaps now we will have to take this seriously, and it is beyond belief that some people – and some of them in places of power and influence – still think that it's another example of 'fake news'. We are indeed living in very strange times.

But while the fires rage in the Greek islands, my mind goes back to the best holiday I ever had in that part of the world. In the early 1980s, a few of my friends who had some sailing experience persuaded me and my brother Huw Ceredig to join them on a flotilla holiday, starting from Ródos (Rhodes). There were about ten of us on two yachts, and we all met in the harbour at Ródos. It was there that we picked up the yachts and met the rest of the flotilla, but after a day or so we were free to go our own way, as long as we met up with the rest after a week, and again at the end of the fortnight. The beauty of that holiday was that you chose your own course, and decided where you wanted to anchor and go ashore. We slept, and ate sometimes, on board, but did most of our eating and drinking on land at whatever place we decided to call at. The tavernas were pretty basic, but the welcome was always warm, and the food – mostly fish

– was interesting, to say the least. We ventured from the Greek islands to Turkey for a few days, and it was there, deep in a forest, that we met a Kurdish family living in a makeshift tent, and they shared their meagre food with us, and even gave us the only cucumber growing in their little garden, watered by a hosepipe which seemed to stretch for miles. The young son was captivated by the only book we had in our possession – the yacht's log book, which we'd been warned to guard with our lives. The young boy wanted that book more than anything in the world, and we felt so bad that we couldn't give it to him. That was my first encounter with the Kurdish people, one of the most maltreated nationalities in the world, and it is a relationship which I have kept up to this day.

Over the years, I've been blessed with opportunities to see many countries, and most of these chances have come directly or indirectly through my singing, and many of them through doing television programmes about other countries. I wrote a song during the terrible Ethiopian famine and drought in 1984, '*Hawl i Fyw*' (The Right to Live), which has become one of my best-known songs, and one of the songs the audience always join in the singing of. A few years after the famine, we did a programme about the work of WaterAid and Christian Aid in Ethiopia, and the experience is one I will never forget. Though the effects of the famine were still evident, and despite the obvious poverty, wherever we went, we were greeted with smiling people and laughing children. There is no doubt in my mind that their strong religious faith plays a large part in their ability to cope with great

106

adversity. But the most vivid memory I have is of a young boy on his way to school listening transfixed to a recording of *'Hawl i Fyw'* on our car stereo. The others had gone out filming, leaving me in the back seat looking over my links, with the door wide open in the heat. The lyrics are written as if spoken by a boy filmed during the famine, his face filling our TV screen, and the song asks what happens when the camera goes away. The boy on his way to school that day could well have been the boy in the song, and he listened as if he understood every word. When the song ended, I had tears in my eyes and he went on his way along the long, dusty road to school. Whenever I sing the song, I always think of him, and wonder what became of him in a country plagued by constant famine and wars.

As I cast my mind back over the years, there are many standout memories. Taking part in a singing festival in San Sebastian soon after Franco's death, the velodrome venue was a cauldron of passions as the young Basque people enjoyed freedoms which had been denied them under Franco's regime, like the right to fly the flag of the Basque country, and to sing their own songs in their own language. Franco's policy was to prevent Basques from policing their own country, and all singer-songwriters had to submit their songs for approval by the Spanish authorities. But as the police didn't understand Basque language, one singer told me that the way around that was easy: he gave the police a list of permitted songs but sang completely different ones, and the police were none the wiser – though they probably wondered why the audiences reacted so passionately!

I have many vivid memories of a visit to Patagonia to film another programme for S4C. I must confess that my feelings for Patagonia are mixed – but not in a negative way as far as the people who live there are concerned. The Patagonian story is one of great heroism and of survival in the face of adversity, and I have nothing but admiration for their tenacity and their faith. My doubts are about the whole principle of building a 'New Wales' on other people's territory – which of course is the story of the United States, Canada, Australia and New Zealand as well, and it would be churlish to single out the Patagonian Welsh for criticism for doing what millions of others were doing at the same time.

To return to our experiences there, the first memory is of my first day in the town of Gaiman. I was walking along the street when a car pulled up in front of me, and a lady jumped out to thank me for the songs on the *Cwm Rhyd-y-Rhosyn* albums, as they had helped her to raise her daughter to speak Welsh. I had to pinch myself, as I was still suffering from jet lag after the long journey by air to such a far-flung land! The second memory comes from the western reaches of Patagonia, in the foothills of the Andes, when a Spanish-speaking café owner sang my song to Victor Jara, the patriotic Chilean singer killed by Pinochet after the 1973 *coup d'état*, in Spanish.

The other lasting memory was of our last night there, and singing in a hall often used for community concerts in Welsh and Spanish. I had to finish with '*Yma o hyd*' of course, and I confess that it was the most challenging performance I have ever given of the song. For whatever message the song conveys to us who live in Wales, can you imagine what it conveys to the descendants of those who risked their lives to create a Welsh-speaking self-governing enclave in South America? When they sing "despite everyone and everything, we are still here", they sing from deep down in their souls. I will never forget the strength of the emotion filling that room in Gaiman that night.

CHAPTER 9

Politics and Religion

I'M A POLITICAL animal in the sense that I am passionately concerned about the way my country – and my world – is run. And I believe that everyone should be concerned about, and involved in, the way things are run. That, to me, is the essence of democracy – that everyone should play a part in the way our lives are being affected. Politics is not something for someone else – those men over there in grey suits – politics is for us, all of us.

Unfortunately, that is not the way it is. Politics has almost become a dirty word for the way a handful of people are running things for their own good, and not the general good. What has happened to the political scene in London and America over the past few years – the terrible era of Trump and Johnson – has made me sick at heart, and has alienated the people from the democratic process. This is so bad for the future. For my part, the answer is to create a new way of doing things here in Wales, to get people involved in their own communities, working with an independent, decentralist government elected by the people of Wales, and answerable to the people of Wales. We have the resources, and we have the ability, to create a sustainable society where diversity and equality go hand in hand, and where the traditional values of our culture are appreciated. The new Wales of the future will not be a carbon copy of the past, but an adventurous, forward-looking and outward-looking nation, proud of its past, and confident in itself. I truly want to be part of that new Cymru.

But having high ideals isn't enough. We have to get stuck in. And that's when it becomes difficult. Sitting in a bleak room working through the latest Community Council agenda, or listening to county councillors talking a confusing mixture of crap and sense, or arguing about a planning application for a barn conversion – these are not exactly the kind of experiences that fill you with excitement for the future. But someone has to do it, and over the years I have tried to do my share, and I have the scars to prove it. I began this treacherous journey in 1974, barely three years after my first spell in prison, while I was still a fairly active member of Cymdeithas yr Iaith, and editor of its monthly magazine *Tafod y Ddraig* (The Tongue of the Dragon), when I stood in the General Election as a candidate for MP for Ynys Môn.

I was up against the old stalwart Cledwyn Hughes, who had served the island well for many years and was so much a part of the scenery that he didn't have to canvass for votes. Nevertheless, I received a warm reception from the *gwerin* (working people) of the island, and indeed began to think I could win; but as the election approached, especially during the last week, my support ebbed away at an increasing rate and people openly said that they couldn't bring themselves to vote against old Cledwyn. So I lost, but got a respectable vote, and I believe began the process which eventually led to Ieuan

Wyn Jones' victory there. The second General Election of 1974 was a nightmare for me, as for some reason the Plaid candidate who preceded me made it known that he would be standing again in the following election, and my band of canvassers disappeared from sight. In the final analysis, Anglesey is an island, and a candidate from outside stands no chance against a native islander. Politics is pretty basic, and often brutal.

In the following year, however, I stood in my own village of Waunfawr for the District Council and won unopposed, which led to four enjoyable years dealing with housing and planning matters and the inevitable flow of complaints. We pushed for a new policy of buying existing properties and refurbishing them as homes for local people – the policy we were already operating successfully in Cymdeithas Tai Gwynedd. This was against the grain of the housing officers and their masters in Caerdydd, but we managed to get it done for a period, which provided affordable homes within the existing community. But this was my first taste of the inflexible attitude of most planners, who have been raised in the English tradition of Town and Country Planning. However, my first experience of council duty came to an abrupt end in 1979 when a village stalwart of the old guard stood as an independent against me. Although I got exactly the same percentage as Dafydd Wigley, who retained his Caernarfon seat in the General Election on the same day – 49% – it was not enough to win, as the supporters of all the other parties went for the independent. So my first stint as a councillor came to an end.

With Thatcher ensconced in Number 10, Wales began to feel the heavy hand of Thatcherism. One of the most flourishing factories in our area was bought by an asset stripper and closed, despite its long profit-making record, and its host of highly skilled and experienced workers. They were told to move to another of the firm's plants in England if they wanted a job. The cruel reality of Thatcherism blew through the Welsh coalfields, threatened the steelworks, and put pressure on the Welsh family farms. They were grim times, and for me personally the Eighties developed into a decade of sad upheavals. They began with two successful concert tours with the folk group Ar Log, but then gradually descended into a series of storms: I was imprisoned in the Welsh-TV-channel campaign, my marriage fell apart, my father died from a heart attack, I lost a European election as the candidate for the North of Wales, lost a Plaid election for the Presidency against Dafydd Elis-Thomas, and I moved into a terraced house in Caernarfon, near my children's school so we could keep in touch. Luckily by 1988 things were looking up again: I had a 25th singing anniversary concert in Corwen, married Bethan, and started doing gigs with the Band. It began to feel like a new beginning.

The mid Nineties saw another rearranging of Welsh local authorities, this time doing away with the District Councils and incorporating their functions into the new counties – of which there are 22, compared to the 8 larger County Councils under the previous regime. Gwynedd was reduced in size, and Ynys Môn became a single unitary authority. I managed to win the Bontnewydd seat from the councillor who had been there for many years, and so began an exciting time for Plaid Cymru, running the new Gwynedd unitary authority, and appointing a new group of officers and staff. Our main achievement was to make *y Gymraeg* the first and main language of operations, and this I believe has been the most important development in the status and use of the language in history. For the first time in centuries, Welsh would be the main medium of government in this large part of north-west Wales, and any translating would be from Welsh to English, and not vice versa. Cymraeg would now be the norm. Of course, there were teething troubles, and a few members of staff tried to take us to court. But we managed it, and the most pleasing aspect of the whole exercise was seeing members of staff managing to improve their Welsh to such an extent that they could answer questions in meetings fluently in Welsh within a matter of weeks. For the first time in modern Wales, our language had the law and authority firmly on its side.

In 2003, I stood for the Presidency of Plaid Cymru against my old friend Cynog Dafis, and managed to win. But the victory was fraught with difficulties. For a start, this was the first time since the Sixties that the party had had a President and Leader who was not an MP or an Assembly Member, and neither I nor the party had fully appreciated the problems that could arise from this. I didn't have a team of staff members working for me, and had to sustain myself by working elsewhere; Ieuan Wyn Jones – leader of the Plaid group in the Assembly – on the other hand, had a team of full-time assistants. I was half-promised the services of a PR person, but even that didn't materialise and I was left pretty well alone as a party leader. I travelled every week to the Plaid group meeting, but it became evident very soon that the arrangement wasn't sustainable, and that Ieuan, as leader of the group, was the only one who was in a position to operate as leader.

So the Presidency changed to being a leader in name only, and I concentrated on acting as a link between the elected members and the grassroots of the party. I think I performed that task well, and I still feel the party needs someone in that role – which could perhaps avoid the present problems in the Bay bubble. The strength of Plaid Cymru lies with the ordinary members in their communities throughout Wales, and the link between them and the Senedd in Caerdydd must be strengthened. We cannot afford to be just the party of elected members, and those members (excellent as they are) must be seen often and regularly in their constituencies. And I long for the day when the number of Senedd members can be increased so that they can do their job – and operate in their dual role in the Senedd and at grassroots level – more efficiently.

So my tenure as President of Plaid Cymru, although it was a period free of any major internal wrangling, was not an altogether successful one. It gave me a taste of the less congenial side of politics, which convinced me that I was right in my decision to stay out of Westminster and Cardiff Bay government. But I believe there's a more fundamental reason why I could never be a 'successful' politician: I don't think in terms of power. I'll speak in the next chapter about the power of songs, but that's a completely different sort of power. In fact, I don't think I fully understand the concept of political power, and as far as I can see, every successful career politician needs a yearning for power: that's what drives them. And I don't use the term in a derogatory sense – they have an instinctive sense of how to achieve power, and how they'd use that power to further their cause. As we all know, power can be used for good or evil, and sometimes it's not easy to tell the difference. Some politicians have exercised their power in a negative way, and have been applauded for their resolve and grit, regardless of the outcome. Maggie Thatcher was 'The Iron Lady' who was not for turning: she knew what power was and what she wanted to do with it, and was determined to achieve her goals, come what may – but did she use her power for the general good? I doubt it very much!

I remember when I began to realise that I had no real notion of power. I was leading the Economic and Planning portfolio on Gwynedd Council and an MP told me one day, "Do you realise that you have far more power than I have in planning matters?" I looked at him aghast, as the thought that I had real power had honestly not crossed my mind. For me, being chair of the Planning committee was a job, a responsibility; I was a cog in the wheel of democratic government, and even though I was called upon to make quite key decisions from time to time, ultimately the power lay with the elected members as a whole. I used to enjoy the old way of putting motions forward, discussing the point, occasionally getting into quite heated arguments, but then putting it all to the vote to settle the matter, and the side that got most votes won. But Tony Blair put a stop to all that, forcing all unitary councils to elect a cabinet with 'scrutiny committees' which are supposed to keep them in check (but rarely function well). In reality, the cut-and-thrust of democratic argument went out of the window, and most of the important decisions are taken by a small number of cabinet members, all because Blair wanted to better manage and control his Labour-run councils. It was so much easier for him to control a few Labour council leaders than a gaggle of quarrelsome councillors, many coming from union backgrounds where argument for argument's sake was the order of the day.

In the final analysis, democracy is the only good system we know. But it isn't a smooth-running machine. It's slow, cumbersome and expensive, and has to allow for the rogue element in society. It has to allow for the elected windbag of a councillor who doesn't always fully understand planning laws, but has the ear of his constituents and has a fundamental right to express their grievances, even though they might be misplaced. The frustrations and delays we often experience in local government is the cost we have to pay for a functioning democracy. It will never be perfect, and will never be swift. But the alternative is very much worse – the ever-increasing power of corporations and big companies encroaching on our lives, and influencing more and more of our public services, aided by politicians who wield their power purely for personal and selfish ends.

My role as a county councillor came to an abrupt end in 2008. After 13 years of serving my community as best I could, I was thrown out by a combination of factors, the main one being my support for the radical reform of Gwynedd primary schools. Every local authority which has a myriad of small rural schools faces the same problem: as people choose to move from the countryside to the towns, and as more and more young families have to move from rural counties to the cities to find work, the numbers of children in some of the smaller schools fall to such an extent that pupils are stuck with the same teacher for years, and many activities, such as team sport or group singing, become impossible. There is also the financial side, which in Gwynedd in 2008 meant that the average spend per pupil in larger schools was around £2k, while the spend per head in the smallest schools was way more than £10k. But the main argument for reform, in my mind, was the need to improve school buildings to conform to sustainable standards, and to provide modern facilities for all Gwynedd children. We advocated creating *Ysgolion Bro* (Area Schools) where it was viable, Federal Schools in other areas – where three or four schools would be run under one administrative head, leaving the teachers free to concentrate on teaching – and amalgamating other schools, which made the closure of some schools inevitable. This reform had been talked about for decades, and supported by one Education Director after another. But the members knew it would be unpopular, and ducked the issue, time and time again.

We decided to grasp the nettle, and published a long-term plan showing how the schools of Gwynedd would look in about 25 years. We should have played a craftier game, and started with a few localities where there was an obvious need for reform. But we believed we should be more open and honest with the public, and take a bold step towards the future. Of course, all hell was let loose, and those of us who were ready to lift our heads above the proverbial parapet caught the full blast of public anger. I'd been advised by a few old heads on the council staff to step back and let the officers take the lead. But that isn't the way I do things, and I paid the price.

It was another of those periods of my life when I saw how nasty people can be over an issue which touches them personally. There were marches where children carried pictures of me through the streets as the devil behind it all, and I saw friends shouting obscenities at me when they saw me entering the council chamber. The hatred of the Investiture period had returned, but this time, I was amongst my own people. The extreme reaction from all parts of the county led to the formation of a new party – Llais Gwynedd (The Voice of Gwynedd) – and it won several seats, including my own. Most of the leading members of Plaid on the council lost our seats, and Llais Gwynedd became the heroes of the hour. They continued to oppose any reform of schools, and opposed virtually everything else Plaid Cymru proposed for the next decade, but never produced any kind of practical proposals of their own. They acted as a negative force on the council for many years (akin to the UKIP members in the Welsh Assembly), but I am pleased to say that they are no more. Like the UKIP members, they did their worst, and then disappeared like the morning mist.

As I walked to the count that fateful morning, I knew I was going to lose, and what I saw on my way to town was a large banner on the Twtil bridge saying *'Dafydd Iwan, Dos i Ganu'*. Now, that literally means an innocuous 'Dafydd Iwan, Go and Sing", but it's a Welsh idiom which is nearer in meaning to 'Go to hell'. My first thought was that my sons Caio and Celt, who were 15 and 17 at the time, would have seen the banner on their way to school, and I felt sick. I went to the count, duly shook hands with my conquerors, and went home to a sad house. Two things I did as a result of that gloomy day. One was that I released an album with the title song *'Dos i ganu'*, which became very popular, and which pleased my youngest, Celt, for turning a possible personal disaster into a success, with a smile on my face. The second action was standing for the Plaid presidency again, not because I really wanted the job, but because I wanted to prove that I could still win! I felt I had something to prove to myself. I ran an energetic campaign, and won.

Politics has played a huge part in my life. Not only because of my involvement with Plaid, but also because of the way my own politics have shaped me as a person and dictated the direction I took in life. Something else I could say the same of is religion, which has been a constant presence in my life since my childhood, as the son of a minister. They always say you should avoid talking politics or religion – well, we've broken that rule on one score, so I may as well be hanged for a sheep as a lamb and discuss the second one now!

Most Sundays I travel to some chapel or other to lead a service. Most of these are small rural chapels which have seen their congregations gradually diminishing over the years and are now struggling for survival, and I feel I have a duty to support them. Chapels have played an enormous part in our culture and way of life in Wales – it's there that we learnt to sing, to read, to take part in public gatherings. It was chapels, with their Sunday School and Band of Hope, who gave us the great stories of the Bible, and it was there we first heard of the great Christian reformers and revolutionaries, from Jesus through to Dietrich Bonhoeffer, Martin Luther King and Desmond Tutu. But now we're seeing this great tradition in rapid decline, with chapels closing one after another, and the aging remnants of what was once a dynamic force in our communities reluctantly closing their doors for the final time. It's a sad picture, but I cannot turn my back on the ones who are still struggling to carry on, for there is still, amongst the ashes of a dying culture, a spark of life, a flame still burning.

We mustn't confuse this dying culture with Christianity! What we're witnessing is the final decline of a tradition, a way of life, and whenever that happens in a culture, a new tradition will emerge. There will no doubt be a new way of doing things which will bring the power of Jesus' vision of positive love into the mainstream of modern life in Wales. I'll never forget an invitation I received some years ago to lead a service in a small chapel in Ynys Môn. The message over the phone went something like this: "*Dydan ni ddim yn rhyw dduwiol iawn, ond rydan ni'n meddwl y byd o Iesu Grist* (We aren't very pious, but we think the world of Jesus Christ)." The words struck an immediate chord with me, for that's exactly my own approach. I have no time (or much understanding perhaps) for theology and the theories surrounding divinity – the kind of arguments which gave rise to all the myriad denominations we have in Wales – but I think the teachings of Jesus are as sound a basis for human life as any. And where they excel over the other great thinkers (like Marx, for instance) is that they treat the person as a combination of body and soul, and not merely as a physical being. Our goal as human beings is to strive for a better life, not just for material reasons, but to achieve peace, happiness and freedom – and these goals have as much to do with the soul as they have to do with the body.

But before I slip too far into preaching mode, let me try and explain this in more practical terms. I believe the Christian faith is a way of directing our lives in this world, and the underlying concept is that of love – the most positive force in the world. If we want to create a world free of wars and hate, we must change our way of thinking, and believe in the positive power of love. Instead of spending millions of pounds on building weapons of mass destruction (yes, those nasty things that made us go to war with Iraq because we thought Saddam Hussein had them), we should be investing in peace – spending money on an alternative way of doing things, as an alternative to thinking that the problems of the world can be solved by violence and wars. Perhaps the answer will come from the all-engulfing threat which is now upon us: global warming. As it threatens all of us – rich and poor, and all the world's nations – we'll have to come together to change the way we do things. This terrible common threat could well be our saving grace. But that may be too much wishful thinking.

In the meantime, while we endeavour to find answers to the global warming crisis, there are practical steps we can take in Wales to make the Christian church more effective, and more relevant. I was a strong supporter of the move – unsuccessful as it turned out – to merge the denominations in Wales: very few members of the various churches know what the difference between Presbyterian, Baptist, Congregational, Wesleyan Methodist and all the other denominations is, apart from a few obvious traditions like the method of baptism. After turning down the opportunity to join forces, we have overseen the gradual demise of all chapels and churches. There are some exceptions where a few chapels have come together to share a minister or a building, but it's all very haphazard and unplanned.

What we need is to make a concerted effort to wind down the various organisations (easier said than done!), decide which chapel and church buildings are capable of modernisation and being adapted into multi-purpose centres, and develop a Christian church which is proactive in community participation and providing practical support for those in need – the poor, the homeless and the lonely. This should not be a matter of doing the work of government and social services, but should be seen as a natural extension of the Christian faith. After all is said and done, Jesus himself was not too keen on church authorities and rule-makers – he hated the way the Pharisees had turned the word of God into a plethora of rules and regulations. They'd turned the creed of positive action into a million "Thou shalt not..."s. We've been in danger of a similar negative attitude. Meanwhile, I'll still fill most of my Sundays with visits to what's left of a great tradition, hoping to promote these ideas of mine about the relevance of the Christian faith in today's Wales, and today's world.

CHAPTER 10

The Power of Song

I'VE BEEN AWARE for most of my life that songs can be a source of power. Even on a fairly superficial level, when Welsh people come together, the urge to sing is almost instinctive. We call upon our repertoire of songs from school, football and rugby clubs, Urdd camps, eisteddfodau, youth clubs and chapels to enjoy our joint efforts, and if there are members of a local choir amongst us, then we show off our harmony skills as well. I do realise, in saying this, that it's mostly a male-orientated thing, and it often – especially if we're away from home, attending an international match perhaps – involves some degree of macho showing off. Indeed, we deserve the reputation we have as a rowdy, if good-spirited, nation. During the Euros in France in 2016, this reputation was enhanced and widely enjoyed by others, thanks to the exuberant Red Wall fans who followed the team during those heady days.

As a singer-songwriter, I've always been fascinated by the effect some songs can have on the listener, and also on audiences – and here we have to treat the individual listener differently to the crowd. The lone listener often concentrates on the words – or at least the words are just as important as the music or the overall effect – and identifies with the message the song conveys. This can be a serious message, or just a passing whimsy, but the listener engages with the song in a very personal way. And perhaps the ultimate proof of this for a singer-songwriter is when someone comes up to you after a concert and quotes a line from a song, saying something like, "You have no idea what those words mean to me." That's when you start to realise that a song is more than what you created some time ago – a song can grow a meaning and a message you as the composer had no idea about when you wrote it.

But then when we consider the audience as a whole, we talk of a very different effect, and here the audience reaction makes the song into something totally different again. And this is what's happened with 'Yma o hyd' – it's grown into something very much bigger than the song I composed 40 years ago. I cannot fully explain this, but it's a combination of the music and the words, and also by now the Welsh national context, and the radical patriotic message it conveys. But the underlying message is simple and powerful – we have to survive, whatever happens around us. Survival is paramount.

I've received many messages since the song became known through its adoption as Wales' official World Cup anthem, and those messages have come from all over the world. I'll quote one which I believe sums it all up in a particularly powerful way – it's an e-mail from Don Cox, who lives in Michigan, USA:

> In hearing your song, I was first amazed at how beautiful the Welsh language is. No matter how my feelings are,

music is the ONE constant that has always been in my
life...

But then I found a version with the English translation.
Ever since finding that version, I have listened to the
song at least 4 or 5 times every night and just cry. It is
SO beautiful. What gives me hope is the "We're still here
today" message, which is the ONE thing positive I can
now tell myself every morning when I wake up... "I'm still
here today"...

Secondly, the verse regarding the "darkness all around
us" and being "ready for the dawn" is SO powerful. I know
the song is not written about depression... But I must tell
you it fits SO well and this is a song I have personally
found as a life-saver.

Messages like this move you to realise that a mere song
can be so much more than words and music, and all we
composers can do is to humbly accept that we're part of
something we cannot fully understand, but which is an
important part of the human experience. When I came
across the songs of Chilean singer-songwriter Victor Jara,
I soon realised that they meant so much to the people of
Chile, who were suffering under an oppressive regime. He
was a great supporter of President Allende, and paid for
that support with his life after being tortured by General
Pinochet's thugs in the stadium in Santiago in 1973. After
reading his widow's book about his life, I wrote the song
'Cân Victor Jara' to commemorate his life, his inspiration
to his people and his death at the hands of Thatcher's
friend Pinochet. James Dean Bradfield of the Manic Street
Preachers has released an excellent album as a tribute to
Victor Jara, and he asked me to take part in a podcast
about the great Chilean singer-songwriter. One of the

proudest moments of my life, and the first time I realised that 'Yma o hyd' had a life beyond my gigs, was when I read in a London Sunday newspaper that it was James Dean Bradfield's choice of the most passionate song he'd ever heard. Perhaps I will have that carved on my Welsh slate tombstone!

The political journey of my songs is a bit complicated, and yet very simple. I started using melodies from American collections like *The Burl Ives Song Book* (a veritable Bible of simple, singable songs), *Folk is Fun* and other collections by Alan Lomax, and songs by Woody Guthrie and Pete Seeger, and put Welsh words to them. These were usually songs of love, children's songs, or rather innocent patriotic songs. When I ventured to put words and music together myself, I started with the more stridently patriotic '*Wrth feddwl am fy Nghymru*', which explains the four cornerstones of my nationalism – Wales' history, the threat to its language, the drowning of Tryweryn, and 'now it's our turn to do something about it'.

Since that first effort, the patriotic/nationalist songs that followed arose from specific campaigns (like the campaign for Welsh on road signs, and the campaign against the Investiture) or specific incidents, or were inspired by individuals whom I either admired (like Gwynfor Evans) or disliked (like Margaret Thatcher). Sprinkled among these were more lighthearted songs, fun songs, and songs for children. If you make a living – or part of your living – from singing, then you must have a varied repertoire, so that you can vary the songs to suit the audience. You cannot expect people to pay to hear you sing if all you do is preach to them, so you have to mix some jam with the medicine, and always include an element of humour. If I set out to take a swipe at a politician who was diametrically opposed to me – like Maggie Thatcher – the songs would usually be satirical and tongue-in-cheek, as I felt that was more effective than an outright attack, and my songs about royalty have always used the feather rather than the hammer. Children's songs are often the most useful part of my repertoire, as children will frequently be part of my audience, and visits to schools are becoming more numerous since the '*Yma o hyd*' explosion.

After a few years of singing with Edward Morus Jones, a dyed-in-the-wool teacher who used songs and music as an integral part of his teaching methods, we decided to record an album of songs for children in 1974. It was all very informal, and we asked a few musical friends to join us at the secondary school in Blaenau Ffestiniog to record whatever songs Edward and I came up with. Edward arrived, carrying a pile of songbooks, and we set about recording a mixed bag of songs from memory, songs from Edward's books, and a few of our own composition. There were no arrangements prepared, so everyone made up their own accompaniment on the spot, and this is what gives that first collection a fresh, spontaneous sound which still appeals today. Over the next 15 years, Edward and I recorded a total of 67 songs on four albums which still sell to this very day – now available as two-CD packs. It's a collection we're very proud of, and a handy treasury of Welsh children's songs old and new.

Part of its secret as a collection is that each song is introduced by a little story, setting it in the context of an imaginary valley called Cwm-Rhyd-y-Rhosyn (The Valley of the Ford of the Rose), based on the attractively named valley between Llanbrynmair and Llanerfyl in Sir Drefaldwyn, Cwm-Nant-yr-Eira. I remember once I was asked to sing at an end-of-term Christmas dinner in Neuadd Pantycelyn, the Welsh-language hall of residence at Aberystwyth University – the kind of occasion that can be a very raucous, drunken affair. As the volume increased and the students clambered on the tables, I turned to the Warden, who sat rather sheepishly at my side, and asked him, "What on earth can I sing to this crowd?" He thought for a few seconds, and then said, "You must remember that they're the children of Cwm-Rhyd-y-Rhosyn, so I suggest you take them back there." And that's what I did – I sang them the songs of their childhood, and it was a spectacular success!

As I travel the length and breadth of Wales, as I've been doing for the last 60 years, I feel I'm keeping in touch with my country. And my songs have been my constant companions throughout that time. I know I sing mostly to Welsh-speaking audiences, but more and more people who don't speak the language are gradually coming to listen and take part – and this is especially true following the football 'Yma o hyd' experience. The power of these songs is the thing that keeps me going, and is the gift I have to give to my country. Not that they are exceptional songs, but they are honest expressions of one person's feelings for Wales – and it's that honesty which I hope is what comes through above all else.

I'm writing this final chapter a few days after my 80th birthday, and I still find it difficult to believe that I've reached this grand old age. The greetings and good wishes I received were truly inspiring, and I'll have to spread the bottles of whisky with care over the next few years! I have so much to be thankful for, most of all my good health and a great family. My brush with cancer was fortunately light, and the tumour was removed before it took hold, and despite having to take my fair share of tablets, I cannot complain because my zest for life remains unabated. My family came to join us for the birthday celebrations, and Miall Ceiriog and Ffredi Twm, the two latest grandsons to join the clan, made sure we looked forward more than we looked back.

So to mark this 80th birthday, and also to mark the 40th anniversary of 'Yma o hyd', and I suppose also to thank Prifysgol Bangor for believing I deserved an Honorary Doctorate in Music, we'll be holding three concerts at Galeri Caernarfon in early November, where the Band and I will be joined by the combined talents of Bwncath, Pedair, Ar Log and Mynediad am Ddim, as well as the stand-ups Tudur Owen, Eilir Jones and Dilwyn Morgan. The original intention was to have a big bash in Caernarfon Castle, but despite Cadw's willingness to work with us, in the end the problems outweighed the advantages, and we went for three nights at Galeri. During our deliberations with Cadw, I learnt something which was complete news to me. For years now, I've been extolling the virtues of Castell Caernarfon, built by an English king to mark the furthest point of his empire, and to keep us Welsh in our place, but recaptured (as it were) through Cadw by the people of Cymru. But how wrong I was! Although run by Cadw, the castle – along with Biwmares and Harlech castles – remains in the hands of the Crown. So perhaps it's for the best that my celebration concerts will be held in the wonderful Galeri, built not by the English Crown, but by Welsh and European funds, based on the vision of a local Welshman.

Among several awards I have gratefully received over the last few years, the latest is the Welsh Music Inspiration Award for my lifetime contribution to Welsh music. Without any disrespect to the uiversities, I think this perhaps is the most meaningful. If I have indeed inspired anyone anywhere through any of my songs, I am a happy man.

On presenting the Welsh Music Prize Inspiration Award to Dafydd Iwan

There is no doubt that this year's winner has inspired. He has inspired singers and songs, but he has also inspired the Welsh to think, to throw ideas around, to take action and to stand up for what they believe in. He's been doing this for 60 years, but now, in his 80th year on Earth, he's inspiring Wales more than ever.

His songs have been sung at political protests, at children's parties, at football games and in chapel. He has always reflected his view of Wales, with justice and peace at the heart of his beliefs. Nobody has done what Dafydd Iwan has done. Sain, the label Dafydd co-founded, is still the biggest and most successful independent label in Wales, with thousands of records released. Without a doubt, the story of Welsh music would be so much poorer without his energy, his vision and his enthusiasm.

Huw Stephens
10 October 2023

Discography

Singles and EPs first released on the Welsh Teldisc label

Dafydd Iwan with Edward Morus Jones

1966 (TEP 861) *Wrth feddwl am fy Nghymru / Wyt ti'n cofio? / Bryniau Bro Afallon / Meddwl amdanat ti*

1966 (TEP 864) *Mae'n wlad imi / Gee ceffyl bach / Crwydro / Mae'r esgid fach yn gwasgu*

1966 (TEP 865) *Rwy'n gweld y dydd / Beth yw'r haf imi? / Hyn sydd yn ofid im / Stôl i ddau*

1967 (TEP 866) *Clyw fy nghri! / Mae geneth fach yng Nghymru / Rhaid yw dal yn ffyddlon / Paid â chwarae efo'm serch / Tyrd yn ddi-oed*

1967 (TEP 867) *Cân yr ysgol / Chwarae â 'nghalon / Pan glywaf gân y clychau / Trwy'r drysni a'r anialwch*

1967 (TEP 868) *Daw, fe ddaw yr awr / Siôn a Siân / Cân y ddinas*

1968 (TEP 871) *Cân y medd / Tri mis o ddathlu mawr / Cân y glöwr / Sam*

1968 (TEP 875) *A chofiwn ei eni ef / Mair, paid ag wylo mwy / Seinier cyrn a chaner clych / Nos ym Methlehem*

1969 (WD 913) *Carlo / Y dyn pwysig*

1969 (WD 914) *Croeso chwedeg nain / Gad fi'n llonydd*

Released on the SAIN label

1969 (SAIN 2) *Myn Duw, mi a wn y daw / Mari fawr Trelêch / Ai am fod haul yn machlud*

1970 (SAIN 7) *Mae 'na le yn tŷ ni / Yma mae 'nghalon / Mr. Tomos, os gwelwch chi'n dda / Peintio'r byd yn wyrdd*

1971 (SAIN 18) *Pam fod eira yn wyn / Weli di Gymru? / Cân y* Western Mail */ I'r gad*

1972 (SAIN 26) *Gorau Cymro, Cymro oddi cartref / Yno yr wylodd efe*

1972 (SAIN C509/H1002) **Yma mae 'nghân**: *Wrth feddwl am fy Nghymru / Daw, fe ddaw yr awr / Mae geneth fach yng Nghymru / Croeso chwedeg nain / Beth yw'r haf imi? / Cân y medd / Gee ceffyl bach / Hyn sydd yn ofid im / Cân y glöwr / Cân yr ysgol / Gad fi'n llonydd / Rwy'n gweld y dydd*

1973 (SAIN 37) *Tywysog tangnefedd / Mae hiraeth yn fy nghalon / Y steddfod beiling / Mae'r llewcyn yn y jêl*

1976 (SAIN C545 /1045D) **Mae'r darnau yn disgyn i'w lle**: *Dos f'anwylyd / Mae'r darnau yn disgyn i'w lle / Mae prydferthwch (ail i Eden) / Dewch i lan y môr / Siarad â ti a mi / Mae rhywun yn y carchar drosom ni / Baled yr eneth eithafol / Dacw 'nghariad (i lawr yn y berllan) / Merch y mynydd / Mynd yn ôl / Cyn delwyf i Gymru'n ôl / Dim ond un gân sydd ar ôl*

1977 (SAIN C708G/1108H) **Carlo and other songs** (with Edward): *Carlo / Bryniau Bro Afallon / Sam / Cân y ddinas /*

Crwydro / Meddwl amdanat ti / Mae'n wlad imi / Y dyn pwysig / Mae'r esgid fach yn gwasgu / Wyt ti'n cofio? / Chwarae â 'nghalon / Trwy'r drysni a'r anialwch / Siôn a Siân / Clyw fy nghri

1977 (SAIN C709G/1109H) ***I'r gad****: Mae 'na le yn tŷ ni / Ai am fod haul yn machlud?* / *Cân y* Western Mail */ Tywysog tangnefedd / Mae'r llencyn yn y jêl / Peintio'r byd yn wyrdd / Yma mae 'nghalon / Pam fod eira'n wyn / Y steddfod beiling / Myn Duw mi a wn y daw! / Mr. Tomos, os gwelwch chi'n dda / Mae hiraeth yn fy nghalon / Weli di Gymru? / I'r gad!*

1979 (SAIN C750N/1150M) **Bod yn rhydd**: *Weithiau bydd y fflam / Cân Victor Jara / Santiana / Teg oedd yr awel / Mari Malŵ / Bod yn rhydd / Baled y* Welsh Not */ Peidiwch gofyn imi ddangos fy ochr / Penillion i Gilmeri / Mae'n disgwyl / Hwyr brynhawn*

1980 (SAIN 86S) *Magi Thatcher / Sul y Blodau*

1981 (SAIN C817N/1217M) **Dafydd Iwan ar dân** (live recording with Hefin Elis and Tudur Huws Jones): *A gwn fod popeth yn iawn / Teg oedd yr awel / Ac fe ganon ni / Parodi ar 'Eifionydd' / Magi Thatcher / Mae rhywun yn y carchar / Y dref a gerais i cyd / Pam fod eira yn wyn / Am na ches i wâdd i'r briodas / Parodi ar 'Hon' / Cân serch (i awyren ryfel) / Y pedwar cae / Bod yn rhydd / Cân Victor Jara / Yr hawl i fyw mewn hedd*

1982 (SAIN 95S) (with Ar Log) *Cerddwn ymlaen / Y gelynnen*

1982 (SAIN C852N/1252M) **Rhwng hwyl a thaith** (with Ar Log): *Dail y teim / Maen nhw'n paratoi at ryfel / Abergeni / Y blewyn gwyn / Y pedwar cae / Dechrau'r dyfodol / Ciosg*

Talysarn / Y dref a gerais i cyd / Heol y felin + Ilffracwm / Lleucu Llwyd / Cerddwn ymlaen

1983 (SAIN C875N/1275M) **Yma o hyd** (with Ar Log): *Y wên na phyla amser / Cwm Ffynnon Ddu / Adlais y gog lwydlas / Tra bo hedydd / Laura Llywelyn / Ffidil yn y to / Hoffter Gwilym + Mynydd yr heliwr + Nans o'r felin + Hoffed Jac Murphy / Cân i Wiliam / Cân y medd / Pêr oslef / Y chwe chant a naw / Yma o hyd/*

1986 (SAIN C985N/1385M) **Gwinllan a roddwyd (i gofio'r Tri)**: *Draw dros y don / Can i DJ / Mae'r Saesneg yn esensial / Yr hen, hen hiraeth / Cân Lewis Valentine / Gweddi dros Gymru / Hawl i fyw / Os na fydd 'na Gymru yfory / Cwyngan y Sais / Mi glywaf y llais / Gwinllan a roddwyd (i gofio Saunders Lewis)*

1991 (SAIN C453/SCD4053) **Dal i gredu**: *Draw, draw ymhell / Fel yna mae hi wedi bod erioed / Cân Angharad / Oscar Romero / Esgair Llyn / Cân Mandela / Dal i gredu / Cân i Helen / Cân yr Aborijini / Awel yr Wylfa / Doctor Alan / Cân y fam / Yr anthem Geltaidd*

1993 (SAIN C2062/SCD 2062) **Caneuon gwerin** (collection of folk songs): *Moliannwn / Ar lan y môr / Y ferch o blwy' Penderyn / Titrwm tatrwm / Fe drawodd yn fy meddwl / Mynwent eglwys / Harbwr Corc + Fflat Huw Puw / Rownd yr Horn / Y deryn pur / Ffarwel fo i dre' Porthmadog / Si hei lwli / Bugeilio'r gwenith gwyn / Paid â deud / Trwy'r drysni a'r anialwch / Ffarwel i blwy' Llangywer*

1995 (SAIN C2097A/SCD 2097) **Cân Celt**: *I ble'r aeth haul dy chwerthin? (Cân Celt) / Symudwch y bobol / Daw fe ddaw yr awr / Cân y glöwr / Peintio'r byd yn wyrdd / Pam fod eira'n wyn / Dyn oedd yr Iesu / Gad fi'n llonydd /*

Tywysog tangnefedd / Shili-ga-bŵd / Daeth y llwch yn ôl / Dal i ganu 'Yma o hyd' / Y garreg wen / Cana gân fy Nghymru / Rhywbryd fel nawr / Torri'r cylch o drais

1998 (SAIN SCD 2180) **Y Dafydd Iwan cynnar** (double album with 39 early songs): *Wrth feddwl am fy Nghymru / Cân yr ysgol / Ji, geffyl bach / Dos, f'anwylyd / Mae'r darnau yn disgyn i'w lle / Mae prydferthwch ail i Eden / Dewch i lan y môr / Siarad â ti a mi / Mae rhywun yn y carchar / Baled yr eneth eithafol / Merch y mynydd / Mynd yn ôl / Dim ond un gân sydd ar ôl / Carlo / Bryniau Bro Afallon / Cân y ddinas / Sam / Crwydro / Croeso chwedeg nain / Mae'n wlad imi / Clyw fy nghri / Mae 'na le yn tŷ ni / Ai am fod haul yn machlud? / Cân y* Western Mail / *Mae'r llencyn yn y jêl / Pam fod eira yn wyn?* / *Y steddfod beiling / Myn Duw, mi a wn y daw / Mr Tomos, os gwelwch yn dda / Mae hiraeth yn fy nghalon / I'r gad / A gwn fod popeth yn iawn / Ac fe ganon ni / Am na ches i wadd i'r briodas / Cân serch – i awyren rhyfel / Yr hawl i fyw mewn hedd / Cwyngan y Sais / Bod yn rhydd / Penillion i Gilmeri*

2001 (SAIN SCD 8085) **20 Cân oddi ar 'Bod yn rhydd' a 'Gwinllan a roddwyd'** (CD combining the cassettes *Bod yn rhydd* [750] and *Gwinllan a roddwyd* [985]): *Draw dros y don / Can i DJ / Mae'r Saesneg yn esensial / Yr hen, hen hiraeth / Cân Lewis Valentine / Gweddi dros Gymru / Hawl i fyw / Os na fydd 'na Gymru yfory / Mi glywaf y llais / Gwinllan a roddwyd (i gofio Saunders Lewis), Weithiau bydd y fflam / Cân Victor Jara / Santiana / Teg oedd yr awel / Mari Malŵ / Bod yn rhydd / Baled y 'Welsh Not' / Peidiwch gofyn imi ddangos fy ochr / Mae'n disgwyl / Hwyr brynhawn*

2006 (SAIN SCD 2400) *Goreuon Dafydd Iwan* (best of compilation): *Cerddwn ymlaen / Cân yr ysgol / Gad fi'n llonydd / Weithiau bydd y fflam / Ai am fod haul yn machlud? / Gwinllan a roddwyd / Hawl i fyw / Mae hiraeth yn fy nghalon / Draw dros y don / Mi glywaf y llais / Wrth feddwl am fy Nghymru / Peintio'r byd yn wyrdd / Pam fod eira'n wyn / Y wên na phyla amser / Esgair Llyn / Yr hen, hen hiraeth / Cân Mandela / Mae rhywun yn y carchar drosom ni / Mae'r darnau yn disgyn i'w lle / Yma o hyd*

2007 (SAIN SCD 2576) *Man Gwyn: Ar y Mimosa / Cân Michael D. Jones / Tyred f'anwylyd / Porth Madryn / Y rheilffordd gyntaf / Tua Cwm Hyfryd / Cân y ddwy chwarel / Ynys Ellis / Y Cymro a'r aur / Hollywood / Baled Joe Hill / Merch y breuddwydion / Hwiangerdd Corsica / Yr ynys / Daeth yr awr, daeth y dyn* (for Gwynfor Evans)

2009 (SAIN SCD 2600) *Dos i ganu: Dos i ganu / Tyrd, aros am funud / Mae gen i f'egwyddorion / Mae Cymru'n mynnu byw / Mwstasho y gaucho / Cana dy gân / Cân y milwr / Cysura fi / Ambell i gân / Angor / Amser maith yn ôl*

2012 (SAIN SCD 2675) *Cana dy Gân*: 12-CD box set of 219 tracks + bonus tracks

2015 (SAIN SCD 2731) *Emynau* (hymns): *Gwahoddiad (Mi glywaf dyner lais) / Saron (Ni fethodd gweddi daer erioed) / Navarre (Cyfamod hedd) / Lausanne (Pwy a'm dwg) / Ellers (Pan fwyf yn teimlo'n unig) / Wilton Square (O'th flaen o Dduw rwy'n dyfod) / Agnus Dei (Dof fel yr wyf) / Hen ddarbi (O arwain fy enaid i'r dyfroedd) / Amazing Grace (Pererin wyf) / Berwyn (Tyrd atom ni) / Dim ond Iesu / St. Bees (Cymer Arglwydd f'einioes i) / Theodora (Gwawr wedi hirnos) / Bydd canu yn y nefoedd*

Acknowledgements

I THANK IAN Gwyn Hughes, Noel Mooney and all at FAW for giving me a platform to sing on and the Red Wall for joining in with such passion, Dave Driscoll and Marcus Lawry for watching over me, Carolyn Hodges and Y Lolfa for their valuable help in putting it all together, the photographers for their skill, and Bethan and my family for being there for me.

Finally, a word of genuine gratitude to all the great musicians who have accompanied me along the way: the present Band of Hefin Elis, Pwyll ap Siôn, Euros Rhys, Wyn Pearson and Deian Elfryn, the greatly missed Charli Britton, and so many others too numerous to name, and the wonderful army of sound engineers.

Diolch o galon ichi gyd.

Dafydd Iwan
October 2023

Also from Y Lolfa:

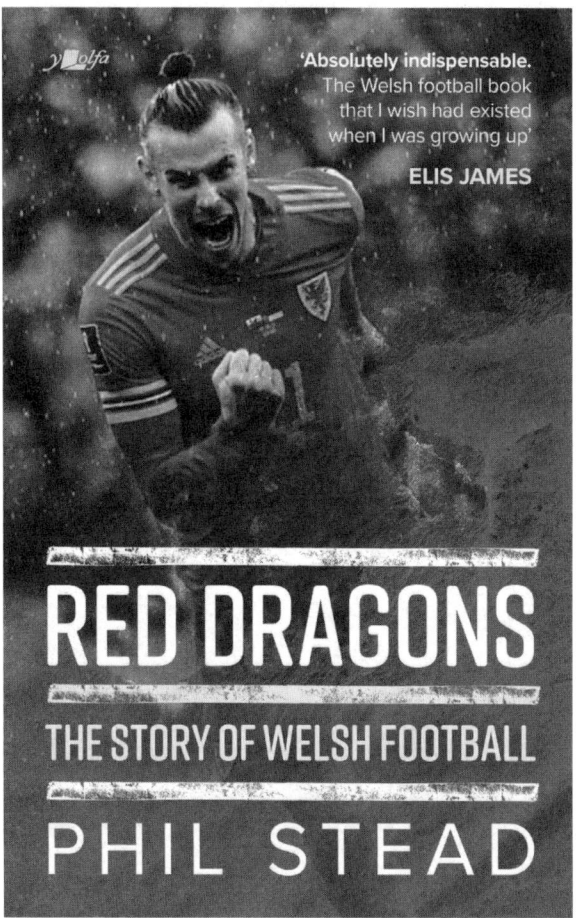

£14.99

The story of Welsh football from its beginnings to the present day, looking at the characters, controversies and development of the country's clubs, players and national team. New, updated 2022 edition, with chapters on Euro 2016 and qualification for World Cup 2022 – the nation's first in 64 years.

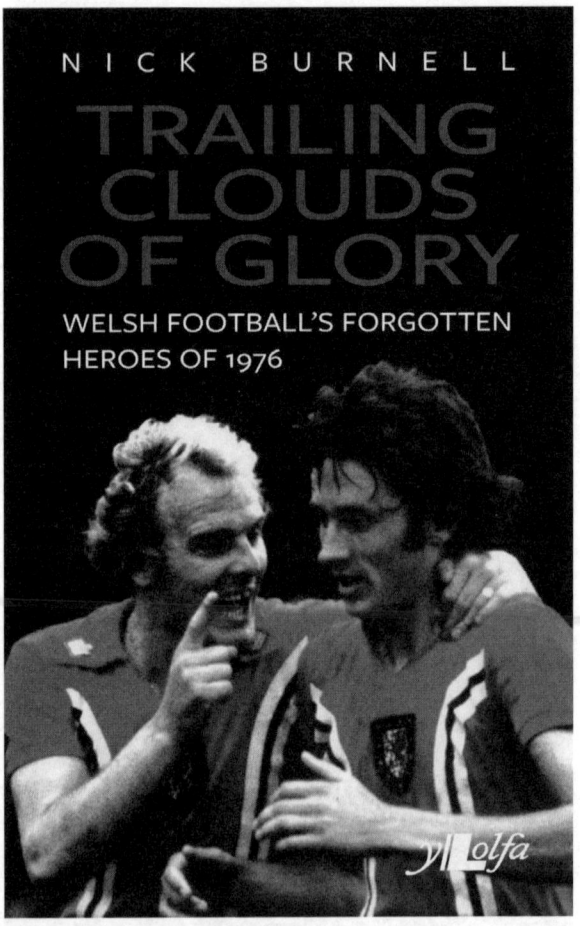

NICK BURNELL

TRAILING CLOUDS OF GLORY

WELSH FOOTBALL'S FORGOTTEN
HEROES OF 1976

y Lolfa

£9.99

Back in the 1970s Wales went from wooden spoon-winners in
the Home International table for four years in a row to Euro 1976
quarter-finalists. This book tells the story of that remarkable
turnaround, including all the matches involved, new interviews
with key figures and a 'Where are they now?' section.

£9.99

Ryan Reynolds and Rob McElhenney's shock buyout of
Wrexham AFC has propelled the club to unimaginable new
global popularity, and the team is finally back in the League
after years in the doldrums. Lifelong fan Peter Read looks at his
own obsessive support, the club's history, and developments
over the first two seasons under the Hollywood stars.

Ask for a print quote!
www.ylolfa.com